He Restoreth My Soul

He Restoreth My Soul

Mary Sturlaugson Eyer

Deseret Book Company
Salt Lake City, Utah

Library of Congress Cataloging in Publication Data

Eyer, Mary Sturlaugson.
  He restoreth my soul.

   1. Eyer, Mary Sturlaugson. 2. Mormons—United States
—Biography. I. Title.
BX8695.S85A33   289.3'3 [B]   82-1363
ISBN 0-87747-908-9   AACR2

Contents

Memories

1   "Afraid?" I quietly asked John. He didn't answer, just kept his hands on the wheel and his eyes on the traffic ahead. After waiting a few minutes, thinking he hadn't heard me, I repeated my question. Still no reply, but from the slight movement of his head I could tell that he had heard me. I then remained silent, feeling a bit disappointed and hurt at his lack of response.

"I could lie and say no," he finally said. "But I won't. I *am* afraid, Mary. But along with that fear is the question of why. Not why am I afraid, but why must things be this way? Why does one human being have to fear another? Why is there so much hatred in this God-given country, this land of plenty? How did such a word or feeling as *prejudice* come to be? Was it due to a lack of intelligence or to a lack of love? Maybe . . . " He paused a few minutes, as if in deep thought. "Maybe it was greed? What was it, Mary, and why?"

I couldn't answer him; instead, I sat searching my own heart and feelings.

"It's hard for me to comprehend an honest reason for prejudice," John continued. "It's hard for me to understand a hatred that can carry one human being to the

1

point of beating up or even killing another. The sad thing of it all is that it has been going on for generation after generation. Why hasn't prejudice been completely wiped out? We are making progress so quickly in other areas; why can't progress truly be made faster in the minds and hearts of people? I . . . "

As I sat listening to John, my thoughts began to wander. I kept hearing his words, "How did such a word or feeling as *prejudice* come to be? . . . a hatred that can carry one human being to the point of beating up or even killing another." As these words pounded at my heart, memories of my earlier life came vividly to mind. Sadness, mixed with guilt, filled my heart as I thought back over the life I had lived while growing up in the South.

Very early in my life I had come to the realization that it didn't matter if I was good or bad, rich or poor; skin color had something to do with the way people treated me. As persecution from whites kept coming my way, a hatred for them began to grow inside of me. By the time I had reached my senior year in high school, this hatred had become deeply embedded.

Our family was large, and as we grew in numbers, we also grew deeper in poverty. It wasn't the hunger that made me hate the white man; nor was it growing up with only rags to wear; nor was it living in a house that was overcrowded, unheated, and without running water. It was the way I was constantly treated like a dog, called names, made to wait till last to be recognized in the stores of the whites, laughed at for the way my hair wasn't straight like theirs, and whatever else they could find to say about me, simply because I was black. It was also for the way I watched my Mama and Daddy being treated and talked to as if they were kids instead of grown-ups— not just by other whites, but many times by their children as they stood and listened. The struggle to survive depri-

2

vation and depression plus racism from a race of people that seemed to have everything—these showed me that they needed to persecute me for my color in order to make themselves feel greater. It was these things plus more that brought about my hatred.

My Mama was very religious. If she could have had things her way, all of us children would have been too. She constantly tried to get us to love all people despite how they treated us. I hated nighttimes because she always bored us to death as she would have us kneel with her for prayer. She would go on and on with her prayers, pleading with the Lord to help us learn how to forgive and forget. I often fell asleep during her prayers, but she still didn't get the hint that I didn't care for God nor her prayers for me.

Because Mama was so religious and Daddy was so strict about our being obedient to them as our parents, we were never able to participate in the riots that often broke out over blacks' being fed up with the degrading treatment they were receiving from the white man. Occasionally I was able to participate in the breaking of the car window of a white who might venture through our neighborhood. My hatred was seldom expressed physically, but verbally I took every chance that came my way.

My senior year in high school brought two significant events in my life. The first was that I was finally able to vent my hatred on a white. A white boy named Doug chose to come to our school that year. My first personal encounter with him came early in the school year. One day I took a letter from my best girl friend that she had written to her boyfriend and began running from her. As I rounded a corner, I ran head on into someone. My notebook hit my lips, splitting the bottom one, and blood began to flow. As I placed my hand to my lip to stop the warm flow of blood, I looked up to see whom I had run into. I was about to apologize when I saw that it was Doug. Instead of apologizing, I began yelling at him. My loud yelling brought students out of their classrooms. One of the black guys, upon seeing my lip bleeding, asked me what had happened. I told him, "That honky hit me." Then I watched as a group of black boys encircled Doug and began pushing and hitting him. Some even kicked him. He probably would have been beaten to death if someone hadn't yelled that the principal was coming.

As I now sat thinking about that event, a lump came to my throat. I recalled how, despite the beating he'd taken that day, his clothes were only slightly ripped and not a bruise could be seen. He'd started past me, then stopped. His eyes were wet with tears, though none fell. "I'm sorry I hurt you," he said. "Is there anything I can do—get you a paper towel or bandage—anything?" I had simply gritted my teeth in anger as I yelled in his face and said, "Just don't let it happen again, honky."

Now my heart broke with sadness at the memory of how I had treated Doug. I closed my eyes tight to fight back my tears. Not wanting John to see me, I quickly tried to think about something happy that had happened in my life. Thoughts of the second greatest event came to mind. Graduation!

Graduation had been the apex of my life. This honor had also brought great joy to my family. I was the first of the twenty-four children to complete high school. Mama was especially happy. She made a dress by hand for me to wear, and that night, following graduation, she and I stayed up and talked till the wee hours of the morning. It was the first time we had ever shared a long conversation. Mama did most of the talking. She shared with me stories about her growing-up days. As I sat listening to her that night, I couldn't help but feel the joy she had

had in giving birth to each of us, yet I sensed that she also wished she had waited longer before getting married and starting a family. She still longed for the chance to go to school and get an education.

Mama had gotten married when she was fifteen, and at sixteen she gave birth to twins. A few years later, following the birth of three more children, she had another set of twins—two sets of twins and twenty single births! Watching her talk that night, I had marveled at her greatness as a mother, for her strength and for the way she always made each of us feel important. That night as we talked, I realized the hope she had for me, a deep hope that I would go forth and make something worthwhile of myself. With that hope, I also sensed Mama's fear—fear that I never would succeed unless I grew to love the Lord and learn how to forgive and love all people. (I knew that to her, "all people" really meant the white race.)

I had received a scholarship to a college in South Dakota. Upon my arrival there, to my surprise I discovered that it was a private, practically all white, Methodist college. My hatred for whites had been intense as I lived in my own little private black world in the ghetto, but it wasn't until I was surrounded by whites in their world that this hatred truly became action.

"Could you have, Mary?"

"Could I have what?" I asked John as I realized he had asked me a question that I'd failed to hear because I'd been thinking about my past.

"Hated to the point of destroying another person?" John quickly glanced my way. As our eyes met, he must have seen the clouded look of sadness that filled my eyes. At the very moment his question was completed, the memories of the two Mormon missionaries who had taught me the gospel in South Dakota came to my mind.

I nodded slowly in answer to his question as I recalled how I had treated those two missionaries. "Yes, I
could have at one point in my life, John," I said. "I really
hated Mormons, and when I told them that if they
bothered me again I would kill them, I really think I
meant it."

Reaching over, John took my hand and squeezed it
tightly. I could tell he was searching for something to say
as he realized the depressing feeling his question had
brought me. I was unable to say more, as I pondered why
those two missionaries had persisted despite the terrible
treatment I gave them when, at that time, they really
didn't have to teach me the gospel. They truly had been
listening to the will of their Father in heaven. Time and
time again they'd knocked on my door to ask me if they
could please share a very special message with me. Time
after time I'd told them, in very graphic language, that I
didn't want to hear their message. After a few months I
realized that language just wasn't going to work, so I began to do violent things to them. When that plan of action didn't work, I wrote a note of final warning to the
elder named Sekona, a note that very pointedly stated
that if they came on the property I lived on one more
time, I would kill them.

I felt myself shiver as I thought about the hatred I'd
had for those two missionaries and the feeling of wanting
to destroy them.

"Are you cold?" John asked.

"No," I replied quickly. "I was just thinking about
what you said about prejudice, hatred, and what it can
drive a person to do. What about you, John? Have you
ever hated anyone enough to want to destroy them?"

I really didn't hear his reply, because my mind had
already rushed back to those two Mormon missionaries. I
thought about how they did not return for a few days af-

ter I had sent that note. The day they did come back, Sarah opened the door and I stood with my mouth open to yell at them, a knife in my hand in throwing position. In what was only a split second, I looked into the eyes of one of them. There was a look there that I could not recognize, but it definitely was not fear. Dropping my hand slowly and shaking my head in total amazement, I simply told them that either they were crazy or I was, and we had best find out. Then I proceeded to invite them inside.

Accepting the message the missionaries shared with me had definitely not been easy. They, like Mama, tried to tell me about a God who loved and cared about me. During the time they were sharing their message with me, I had my mind totally tuned out. Then they said something that really angered me—that we were all brothers and sisters! Mama had tried to tell me the same ridiculous thing, and I just wasn't ready to hear it again.

Later that night, as I thought about all they had said, for the first time in my life I decided to try to find out if there really was a God. My first step was to get out of bed and kneel in prayer, but as I started to do so, I thought about the possibility of Sarah's being awake. Not wanting her to see me praying, I remained in bed and closed my eyes tightly. I uttered words of wanting to know, though my heart was still filled with doubt that there really was a God. Eventually, with the missionaries teaching me and with our fasting and praying together, I gained a testimony and was baptized. At the time of my baptism I still didn't quite believe all that they had shared with me, but with the little faith I had been able to gain, I was willing to trust my all to a God I finally knew did live and did love me—just as Mama had always tried to tell me.

The acceptance of God in my life and my baptism into His true church had cost me my greatest and most prized possession, my family. My brothers felt I was a traitor to my race and my family, and they became deeply bitter toward me.

As time passed, I often felt like an outcast, not just with my family, but also as a member of the Mormon church. I felt like an outcast with my family because they no longer accepted me as one of them. And I felt like an outcast in the Church when I heard speakers constantly stressing the importance of going to the temple and on a mission, neither of which I could do.

Because of the deep love I had grown to have for the Savior, I wanted to share in and be a part of the full blessings of His kingdom. More than anything, I wanted to serve a proselyting mission. Many nights I would lie restlessly in my bed as the desire to serve a mission ate away at my heart. I spent many long hours on my knees pleading with Heavenly Father to please allow me to serve Him as a full-time missionary, but days passed and nothing happened.

As days turned into weeks, and weeks into years, my hope to serve a mission began to lessen. Then, two years later, the Lord granted unto me the desire of my heart. On a hot, but truly lovely, June morning, the word came: *all* worthy male members of the Church could receive the priesthood.

At first I doubted the truthfulness of the words. Then I hoped—hoped that if the words were true, I was not dreaming. As the day wore on, I laughed, I cried, I shouted, I silently and openly prayed words of thanks to my Heavenly Father. With each prayer I felt that my words just weren't conveying to Him what my heart was truly feeling, but now I know that He knew and understood how I felt.

By midday I was talking to President Jae Ballif, who had been my stake president during the times I kept requesting to go on a mission and who was now serving as a mission president in Boston, Massachusetts. I had called him on the phone, but when he answered I was crying too hard to say anything. Somehow he knew it was me, and before joining me in my tears he had managed to utter, "Mary, the Lord was mindful of you and your desire. Go forth and serve Him with all your heart."

After talking to President Ballif, I was about to call President Clarence Bishop, who had been the president of the South Dakota Mission when I was baptized, when the phone rang. "Mary," a male voice said, and it sounded as though he was weeping. "Mary," the voice repeated, and again nothing followed, but this time I was certain of the sobs. Recognizing the voice, I began repeating President Bishop's name. Over and over I said it until I could manage to express the gratitude I felt toward him for not letting those two missionaries give up on me.

I tried to locate Elder Sekona, one of the missionaries who had taught me the gospel, but I was unable to find him. I wanted so desperately to share the joy of that day with him and to thank him for his love, patience, and persistence, and for being in tune with the will of his Father in heaven.

"I love you, Mary," John was saying as I sat smiling from the memories of that happy June 9th day.

"I love you too, John, and I'm *so* deeply grateful to be a member of the Church. The Lord has truly been good to me. Now if He'll only work things out so you can meet Mama," I added, feeling certain that my brothers would prevent it.

"I'm afraid, Mary," John said, "but I love you. No matter what happens to me, I'm going to meet your mother and tell her I love you and want to marry you. Strike out those last few words—I am going to marry *her daughter*." He smiled as he took my hand in his.

"Is meeting Mama what scares you, or is it what she might say?" I asked him teasingly.

Again his silence lasted so long that I wasn't sure if he'd heard me.

"Neither!" he finally answered with conviction. "I'm simply afraid she won't accept me because of what her eyes will see first. And Mary," his voice broke, "being accepted by your Mama is something that's very important to me. I feel she's such a special lady and so close to the Savior that to be accepted by her would be such a choice and righteous blessing," he added in what was almost a whisper.

Squeezing his hand, I searched for words of assurance. I tried to recall things Mama had said about loving one another, but my mind seemed to be completely blank except for the things my brothers had said—and they definitely weren't words of assurance, or even close to it.

More to convince myself, I said, "Don't worry, John, everything will work out. I'm sure they will. Why, who couldn't help but love you at first glance or second or . . ."

"Your brothers!" John said with a quick glance my way. "But I'm not afraid of them." He then flexed the muscles in one arm as he steered the car with the other. "The *only* thing they can do to me," he continued, "is rip my head off and totally mutilate my body. So why should I be afraid? The *only* thing I'm praying for is a quick death from it all."

Though we both laughed, we both knew the possibility of the truth of his statement. Resting my head against the car seat, I again tried to remember some of the things Mama had tried to teach us about love, but this time my thoughts seemed to drift to my mission.

I Know
That My Redeemer
Lives

2   On September 23, 1978, I entered the Salt Lake Mission Home. The night before going to the mission home, I went up to the Provo Temple to spend a few minutes alone. Sitting outside near the water fountain, I realized that my life had been very similar to the rise and fall of the water. I smiled as I remembered the pride and joy my family had all felt the summer I received my acceptance letter to college. I had been the family's first high school graduate, and the thought of my going to college excited everyone. My feelings changed to sadness as I thought of how that pride and joy had turned to so much sorrow and pain. The memories of all that had happened between my family and me in recent years brought tears to my eyes.

Then I thought about the great blessings the Lord had given to my life. Staring at the temple and realizing I could now enjoy the full blessings of it, I thought about other blacks who had joined the Church years before me and who had never seen this blessing come about during their lifetimes. I thought about an "Aunt Jane," a black sister that President Wilford Woodruff wrote about in his journal. He told how she'd come to see him, anxious to go through the temple and receive the higher ordinances of the gospel. He had blessed her for her constant, never-changing devotion to the gospel. When Joseph F. Smith preached at her funeral some years later, he declared that she would, in the resurrection, attain the longings of her soul. Thinking about how she had endured to the end brought a feeling of peace within me. How her spirit must have rejoiced on that very special June 9th!

As I thought about her and her life-long desire, I thought about the many times I'd attended meetings where people had given talks on the importance of the temple ordinances. I remembered the hurt and the empty feeling I'd had as I realized that even though I was a member, the message other than to listen, wasn't for me; the hurt feeling I'd had when counsel was given for the members to pray for the gospel to go forth in other lands, but never for it to go to their black brothers and sisters in this land.

People were beginning to come out of the temple, so I wiped frantically at my eyes and nose. I began to ache for someone to stop and ask me what was wrong or if they could help—anything at all, as long as it would give me an opportunity to share the hurt and the joy that were passing through my life at that moment. But no one stopped. As I stood crying, I began humming, "Sometimes I feel like a motherless child, a long, long way from home." Then I smiled and added, "But I know that my Redeemer lives. What comfort this sweet sentence gives!"

Hours later I drove back to the apartment where I was staying to get ready for the next day. After packing my bags, I felt such depression that I couldn't bear to be alone. Gathering my bags, I drove to the Ellises' and asked if I could spend my last night with them.

The sad, lonely feeling soon lessened as I watched

Dad Ellis patiently trying to chase one of his sons to bed, while the boy kept insisting that his bed was saying its prayers and didn't want to be disturbed.

"You're laughing now, Mary girl," Dad Ellis said to me with a smile, "but just wait until you have some children of your own—then you'll see the fun that's really in it."

As I continued to watch him chase his son, I thought about the time Daddy had caught one of my brothers under the house smoking a cigarette. My brother knew he was in for a beating, so he decided to run so as to gain as much time as he possibly could before getting it. I broke out in a cold sweat, remembering the beatings Daddy gave when we disobeyed him. After that chase, all during my years at home, every time anyone mentioned cigarettes, my brother would break out into tears.

Later that night, lying in bed at the Ellises', I thought again about Daddy and the many times I'd watched him laugh as we played softball or rag ball. Often he'd stop the game and walk over to Mama and tell her he was proud of her for making him the richest man in the world. He would point to each of us and say, "Luk at all the gold mines I's got." He would then hug Mama close—well, almost close, for Mama was usually big with another child. My parents were happy, and that happiness is what they tried to always show us, though we knew there was the fear within each of them of how, and if, we would all survive.

Toward morning, only a few hours before I was to enter the mission home, I turned on my light and made my first entry in my missionary journal. "Dear Daddy," I wrote, "In a few hours I will be leaving the comforts of this home to enter into another dimension of my life. This is something I've wanted to do for quite some time, but, needless to say, now that the time is here, I'm not sure if I want to do it. I miss you, Daddy, and truly wish you were here. It's still hard to believe that you are gone from this earth. It is so very hard to accept the fact that after giving twenty-four of us a chance to come into this world, you have left us. If love could bring you back, you would be right here with me. If loneliness could take me places, I'd be with you. I'm afraid, Daddy . . . a fear I'm sure you must have felt many times in your lifetime. I sure hope I can be like you and not show my fear."

It seemed as if I'd barely closed my eyes again when Mom Ellis knocked on my door to tell me it was time to get up. She opened the door just as I was rolling out of bed to kneel in prayer. Pausing, she stood as if debating whether or not to come in. Finally she came and knelt beside me. A familiar feeling came over me as I remembered the time Mama had come into my room when I was preparing to leave for college in South Dakota. Sitting on the mattress my sisters and I slept on on the floor, I was having very mixed feelings about leaving home for college. Mama quietly came into the room and sat next to me on the mattress. For a few minutes, neither of us said a word. Finally Mama said, "I's real proud of yous, child. Going to college and all. But I's also afraid for yous. I's put yous in the hands of the good Lord, and I's know he's will take care of yous."

"Oh mama, please don't give me a sermon," I said, standing up. "I'm going to be all right, and I don't need your Lord to take care of me."

"Child, yous do need the good Lord. We all do. Someday yous will know what I's trying to tell yous—yous will know," Mama said as she slowly started to stand.

"Mama, I'm gonna go to college, get a good education, and take care of you and Daddy someday. I'm gonna give you everything you have never had. I'm going to buy you a . . . "

"Child, everythang is nothin' wifout the good Lord," Mama interrupted me. She started to leave, then paused at the door, looked at me sadly, and added, "If yous can learn anythang for yo' mama, learn to love the Lord."

I turned and looked at Mom Ellis as I recalled with tears in my eyes the things Mama had said.

"Afraid of the unknown, honey?" Mom Ellis asked. "Just remember," she continued, "the Lord is with you, and He'll take care of you. You will also have thousands of people praying for you each day. Don't be afraid, nor doubt. Okay? And Mary, don't fail to ask for the Lord's help."

I didn't say anything, only nodded my head with understanding. As she left the room I remained kneeling, not uttering a word, just thinking, wondering. Would the Lord really be with me no matter what I encountered? As I thought about the love I now had for Him and His gospel, I remembered the time my brother Roy's car broke down when he was driving to Chicago from Chattanooga. He had to coast to a little town off the freeway. It was winter and a Sunday. Knowing that everything was closed, he sat trying to decide what to do. We didn't have a phone, so he couldn't call for Daddy to come help him. While he was sitting there, a car stopped and a white man about Roy's age got out and walked over to him. Feeling maybe the man would start some trouble, Roy took out his switchblade and sat waiting.

"Car trouble?" the white man had asked.

"What's it to you?" was Roy's reply.

"I wanted to help if I could, plus I don't think it's too safe for you to be here."

"Why'd you wanna help me, whitey?" Roy asked, feeling certain that the man had something else in mind other than helping him.

"Forget it, man. I saw you here and thought you

could use some help." The man got back into his car, and as he drove off he looked at Roy and shook his head. Roy kept his switchblade near, feeling sure the man would return with some of his friends. Darkness started to fall, and fear was building up in him. The car was cold, and Roy knew he couldn't stay in it overnight. As he started to get out of the car the same man drove up again.

"Look, man, it's getting dark, and you've got to get out of here. You can't possibly stay in that car. Where are you going? Maybe I can take you there."

"Why in the ---- are you so anxious to help me?" Roy asked him.

"I'm not anxious to help a nig . . . fellow. I'm just trying to return a favor to some guy that helped me once."

Though Roy didn't trust him, he knew that he had better try to get somewhere for the night. The man drove him back to Chattanooga, which was a little more than a hundred miles. Roy had the man let him out near the freeway, while hoping that no one would see him getting out of a "whitey's" car. The next morning when Roy and Daddy got ready to go get the car, they found it parked out front with a note.

"Didn't have your keys so had to hot wire it. Shouldn't give you any more problems." There was no name, and though Roy never mentioned thanking the man, I wondered if he had considered it and would possibly have done it if he'd known the man's name. But I didn't dwell on that thought much, for Roy's hatred for whites steamed daily.

"Heavenly Father, I now know that it was you watching over my brother, even though he didn't believe in you. Please watch over me too, as I seek to develop faith in you like unto my Mama's."

During my five days in the Salt Lake Mission Home, I made definite promises to the Lord. One of those promises was that no matter what happened to me in Texas, I would endure to the very end. Inside my scriptures I taped a little card as a reminder of that promise. "As a missionary I might suffer long, yet I will be kind and *will not* give up. I will bear all things, endure all things, for I *know* this gospel is *TRUE*."

As I boarded the plane for the Texas San Antonio Mission, I felt the desire to serve a mission burn deeply within me. Resting my head against the seat of the plane, I had to reassure myself that I was actually going on a mission. I was going to be in the service of my God. I thought about Elijah Abel and when he'd served a mission back in 1883. Because he was part black, he had been unable to exercise any priesthood rights during his mission to Canada. How had he felt? Possibly sadness, and yet, a deep sense of gratitude and joy to simply be in the service of his God. I really didn't know why I was now being blessed to have this blessing during my lifetime, but I vowed to truly do my best so that I would not disappoint any of those who had gone on before me nor those that would follow.

Reality hit me. I, Mary Frances Sturlaugson, was actually going on a mission! The reality of it all and the joy that it brought were almost overwhelming. I was going to be in the service of my God. This thought made me think about Mama and how proud she should be; I had finally come to know the God she had tried so desperately to get me to know. As I thought about all of Mama's efforts in the past to teach me about God, I felt certain it really wouldn't hurt her to know that I was serving him in the Mormon church.

The plane ascended high in the sky and I glanced out my window at the heavens. I thought about Heavenly Father and the many times I'd pleaded with Him to grant me this blessing of going on a mission. Then I recalled

President Ballif's words "the Lord was mindful of you, Mary," and a feeling of inadequacy came over me. He had granted me the opportunity to serve this mission. "You must have a lot of faith in me, Heavenly Father," I said to myself. "Before this mission ends, the feeling is going to be mutual."

It Wasn't Easy!

3 My first morning in the mission field, I awoke feeling somewhat apprehensive, knowing I was about to begin my calling for the Lord. I was excited to go door to door and see who was inside those houses, and I also wondered how excited the people would be when we told them about the special message we missionaries had to share.

I'll never forget the first time I knocked on a door. A man yelled harshly, "Just a moment!" He jerked the door open and stared at us, which scared the words I had prepared right out of me. He practically yelled in my face as he asked what we wanted. I quickly began uttering our names, but before I could finish, he yelled at me to "stop all the garbage and tell him what I wanted." He frustrated me to anger as I yelled back that we were Mormon missionaries with a very special message to share. Before I could finish he started laughing.

"I'm white, and I don't believe in that church, and I can't believe I see you standing there telling me you're a missionary for it. Mormons??? That church that has treated your people like the ground I walk on to keep their 'white superiority,' and you now have the audacity to say you are a missionary for them. You need your head examined," he said as he started to step back inside his house.

"Sir," I said, taking one step toward him to block his slamming the door in my face, "I know you and others will see me first as a black, and I know that I am black, but I am also a child of a Heavenly Father who loves me. As his child, I don't have all the answers, especially not for the injustices I have seen going on in this world toward my race, but I do have some answers. I know who I am and what and whom I represent. I know that I have a truth that neither you nor anyone else can make me ashamed of. If you would take the time to listen, maybe you'd find out that my head is okay. But if you want to continue to feel as you do, then to not listen will certainly satisfy your conclusion."

It hurt me deeply to have him laugh at me, and as we walked away I was reminded of the time Daddy took me with him to collect pop bottles in the white areas because my brothers were down with the flu. Daddy and I stood at one door waiting for someone to answer his knock. A kid about the same age as I opened the door. When he saw us he yelled at my Daddy, called us degrading names, and asked what we wanted. Daddy proceeded to slowly and politely ask for the few pop bottles lying near their gate. The kid told Daddy to take the bottles and "don't come bothering us again."

As he slammed the door, I quickly looked up at Daddy with an angry look on my face, wondering why he hadn't taken that boy and beaten the living daylights out of him for talking like Daddy was a kid. Daddy didn't look at me as he turned to go get the bottles. I didn't bother to help him, I just got into the truck. On the way home I could tell Daddy was trying to find words to explain why he had let that happen, but I just sat near my door and stared ahead. I actually hated my Daddy at that moment for letting that boy call us niggers to our face and treat us as if we were nothing. We may have been starving, but did starvation mean having to give up our dignity? When Daddy stopped the truck in front of our house, I turned to tell him how I didn't respect him as a daddy. There rolling down Daddy's face were tears. This angered me even more, and I jumped out of the truck without saying a word and slammed the door as hard as I could.

As my companion and I started up the street for the next house, I realized Daddy had suffered humiliation because he loved us. Now I drew strength and courage from remembering that about him. My companion asked if I would take the next door. She placed her arm around me and said, "Remember the Savior and all He went through for us? It wasn't easy for Him either, but He did it."

As the day progressed, so did the humiliations. I honestly had had enough humiliation for one day. I simply wanted to go home—go home and live a good life.

Lying in bed that night, I wondered why so much persecution had come when all I was trying to do was share a message about the Lord. I even wondered why the Lord had let so much happen when it was Him I was trying to do this for.

As I lay there thinking about all that had been said to me that day, I thought about Martin Luther King, Jr., and the many times I'd watched him getting yelled at and spat upon. Sometimes he was even pushed down and kicked, but he never said one complaining word. He had had a dream, a dream he was determined to reach through love and peace. Now I was able to accept what he had been trying to do and the way he had tried.

"Blessed are the peacemakers: for they shall be

called the children of God. Blessed are they which are persecuted for righteousness' sake: for theirs is the kingdom of heaven. . . . Love your enemies, bless them that curse you, do good to them that hate you, and pray for them which despitefully use you, and persecute you." (Matthew 5:9-10, 44.)

I thought about the persecution I'd gone through that day and the persecution I'd gone through with my family, and wondered if I could be like others who had gone through the same or more than I. As I closed my eyes to sleep, I renewed my promise to the Lord that I would endure to the very end.

As if the humiliation from people wasn't enough affliction, my body decided to give me more, as it broke out in a rash. Tiny blisters spread over my entire body, and I had to scratch constantly. The itching was horrible. During the day and especially at night, I scratched constantly. My body often bled from the scratch marks made by digging my nails into my skin to stop the itch.

One night, after lying in bed for what seemed like hours, scratching and trying to get relief long enough to fall asleep, I finally got up and went into the bathroom. Leaving the light off, I knelt on the floor and cried. While crying, I began to pray. I begged Heavenly Father to please tell me what to do about the rash. I told Him it was really affecting my work and that I didn't want anything to hinder His work. As I was praying, the thought came to me not to scratch when the itching started, but even as the thought came, I continued to scratch. Feeling that the itching wasn't going to stop and that the Lord wasn't going to give me any help, I returned to my bed. As I lay there trying to sleep and to fight the itching, the thought again came not to scratch, but to simply endure the itching. I was about to scratch a place that was already completely raw when again the thought came not to do so. This time I obeyed, though it was pure agony. I don't know how long I lay there crying and wanting desperately to scratch, but somehow I must have fallen asleep.

The next morning as I got into the shower I realized I didn't itch. Looking at my arms and then at the rest of my body, I discovered that the rash was completely gone. There wasn't even a scratch mark to be seen. At first all I could do was stand there with my mouth open in total disbelief; then I dropped to my knees and thanked my Father in heaven.

Realizing what had just taken place in my life, I thought about the time I'd come home from school to that old familiar smell of "no food." My baby brother was crying as Mama sat rocking him. Looking at mama, I could tell she had been crying, too. My baby brother not only was starving, but he was also stuffy with a cold. Mama got up and handed him to me, then went into her bedroom. Feeling angry, I waited a few minutes and then handed the baby to one of my brothers and followed Mama into her room. As I suspected, she was kneeling. Instead of interrupting her, I decided to listen and see what foolish words she was praying to someone who didn't exist. I listened as she told this God of hers how He had delivered His children out of the hands of Pharaoh's army; how He had fed five thousand with five loaves of bread and a few small fishes; how He had healed the sick and raised the dead; how she knew all power was in His hands. And then, like a little baby, she wept. I stood watching Mama weep. Hearing her cry broke my heart. As I started toward her, she began pleading with the Lord to help us, offering Him her own life rather than having her children starve to death.

"Mama, don't leave us," I said, kneeling beside her. "We couldn't make it without you." I wasn't sure Mama heard me because she continued to pray. After a few more words to her God, she was silent. Finally, she looked over at me, pulled me close, and began rocking me in her arms. I had not allowed Mama to hold me ever since my hatred began for her God and his white people. "It's gone be alright, child," Mama said, as she continued to rock me, tears streaming down her face.

When Mama and I walked back into the room where my brothers were, the baby lay cooing to himself, and he was breathing smoothly. The hungry look that had been on my brothers' faces seemed gone as they busied themselves playing some game. A peace and calm filled the air, even a warmness.

At that time I had not accredited the feeling to God, but now as I watched the miracle my body had just gone through I knew it was because of God. Some might not feel this was much of an experience, but to me it was a great miracle. It was also a testimony of faith and prayer. But most of all it was a lesson to me on how thoughts are the teachings of the Spirit, and how miracles can happen when we obey those teachings. That rash made me stop and evaluate myself to see how effective I had been or failed to be in the work I'd been called to do.

That night as I knelt to pray, the words just wouldn't come—only the feeling of how I had failed the Lord in the promises I'd made to Him that night in the Mission Home in Salt Lake City. I had promised Him I would trust my family to His care and that I would trust in Him to work things out between us; yet I worried constantly about them and how I could possibly get them to accept me back into the family. I'd promised Him I would serve Him with my whole heart, might, mind, and strength; yet I was always worrying about me and what I was going through instead of being concerned about the people I'd been called to share the gospel with. Realizing these things, I struggled for words, and after getting nowhere, I got off my knees and crawled into bed.

I was unable to sleep, and the thought suddenly came to me to go jogging. The feeling grew and grew till I was unable to lie there any longer. Quietly I eased out of bed so I wouldn't wake my companion and got dressed in my sweats and went outside. I knew that I shouldn't be alone, but I ignored the thought and got ready to take off running. I'd just taken my first set of steps when I was literally stopped in my tracks—the mission rule of "do not be alone from your companion at any time" was pounding in my mind. With that came the words of President Fisher, my stake president who had set me apart for my mission: "Stay close to the Lord through your obedience." Trembling, I stood there for a moment trying to decide what to do. "Okay, Lord," I finally said, "I won't go off running by myself, but I'm going to stand right here and jog in place until I have found out why I doubt you and how to overcome it. I honestly want to serve you with my whole heart, might, mind, and strength, but I'm really having trouble doing so. Please help me." I then commenced jogging in place.

The nights in Texas are usually extremely warm, and this particular October night seemed warmer than usual. I was more aware of the heat than I was of the tiredness that struck my body every so often. I felt as if my breathing was slowly being smothered, and a few times I had to gasp hard for air. I gradually began to see millions of little stars before me, but I wouldn't stop my jogging. I needed the Lord's help, and until I got it, I would not stop. After what seemed like hours, I suddenly realized what the problem was and who could help. Exhausted, I stopped jogging, sat down on one of the steps with my face in my hands, and cried.

Within me the promise of Eternal Life lies glowing warm, brightening every day. Within me the knowledge that I must endure comes clear to me as He draws near to me. I know now that the life I seek must rise from deep inside. He's given me all I need to reach beyond the skies. Within me the love of Christ surrounds my weak and failing heart, casting strength with faith. And through His loving molding I can finally see His plan; my crown lies in store for me. He will know me; He'll call me by name, and I'll take His hand, feel His love, know His peace, share His joy. On my knees I seek His constant guidance to be with me when I falter close to sin. Though failings come, I know that I can stand the trials set here for me—if I free the bright spirit within me. (Madelyn Tolman.)

The next day we had a zone conference. Elder Dean L. Larsen of the First Quorum of the Seventy was our speaker. We arrived early, and as I sat alone, thinking about last night, Elder Larsen came and sat next to me and introduced himself. He asked me how my mission was going and if I regretted my decision to serve. I shared with him briefly some of the difficulties I had had and the doubts that often came when these difficulties occurred. He nodded with understanding and then, standing to leave, he shook my hand and said, "You made the right decision in coming. This is where the Lord truly has need for you."

My eyes were filled with tears as I watched him slowly walk up to the stand and sit down. The Lord had again assured me of my calling through Elder Larsen. Everything truly did lie within me!

Opposition
in All Things

4 The discouraging times continued, but I kept working to take them in stride and to do my best to give the
Lord my all. I remembered how Kevin, the young man
I'd dated before my mission, had said to take the rough
times and use them to grow closer to the Savior, and as I
applied this advice in my daily life I felt growth. When
people slammed their doors or said rude things, I centered my thoughts on the idea or concept of "What
would the Savior do?" As we approached doors or taught
people the gospel, I prayed fervently, that their hearts
might recognize the truth we bore witness of. I studied
scriptures and memorized hymns, not just Mormon
ones, but ones Mama had sung to us as children. And always, with the love and support of my companion, I went
forth as if everything depended on me, yet knowing I
was nothing without the Lord.

 The gospel became my life. The joy it brought filled
my daily struggles. A warm feeling glowed within me
when I reached out to others and saw something beautiful happen to their lives as they learned and accepted the
true gospel of Jesus Christ. My only regret was a sadness
at not having listened to Mama years ago when she'd

tried to tell me about the Lord and His goodness. I felt I'd cheated myself from the feeling I could have had before.

The members were good to me. Many expressed excitement over the revelation and for my having been called to Texas. Of course, there were times when some showed racist attitudes. One such time was when a man in our ward was going into the chapel and one of the elders and I spoke to him. He continued on as if he hadn't heard us. I spoke again, louder this time. He stopped, slowly turned, and said, "I don't speak to missionaries, especially black ones." Hearing these words was like history repeating itself. So many times I had gone downtown in Tennessee and had been thirsty and wanted to buy something to drink, and the waitresses would argue with one another as to who was going to wait on me, each commenting, "I don't wait on niggers." Despite how I tried to think of myself on my mission as a child of God, many persons let me know that I was black first, and whatever came second really didn't matter that much to them.

The Lord seemed to be about the only person that didn't notice my color, as He continued to guide us daily to people and places where He had need for us. Working with the spirit and guidance of the Lord was one of the greatest and most beautiful experiences I had each day. Though oftentimes we didn't understand why He led us to certain places, we always found out later, if we were patient and obedient to the promptings of the Spirit.

Having promised the Lord I would have total faith in Him proved a valuable promise to have made. I recall only once questioning His guidance after I had made that promise. That doubt came at a time when we had been led into danger.

Having strong feelings that we were to go far into

the country and look for people with whom to share the gospel, my companion and I had followed through on that impression. We found a lady and three children to teach, but on a return visit the father and one of his friends were there. The friend made a very rude remark about me, while the father just stood glaring at me with a look that reminded me of the expressions I'd often seen on the faces of whites when I was growing up. We soon learned that the father and his friend had organized the Ku Klux Klan in that area, and he had vowed that a black person would never set foot inside his home. The owner of the property was also a member of the Klan and had given him permission to shoot "any niggers" caught on the property.

As we learned all this, I recalled the fear and frustration I'd felt as a child. I recalled the many times my father shared with us things the Klan had done to his parents and some of his best friends. The crudest of all had been when the Klan found Daddy and a friend fishing on a lake. Daddy had become separated from his companion for a moment, and upon seeing the hooded men surround his friend, he ran to town to get help. When Daddy and the people he had gotten to help returned, they found his friend with blood pouring out of his eye and his face practically caved in from what must have been someone's foot stomping him. Daddy had constantly warned us to stay away from the Klan because he felt they had absolutely no feelings whatsoever.

As I recalled that experience now, I felt frustration toward the Lord; I questioned him as to why He had guided us into a situation that could have cost us our lives, at least mine. Yet, as I questioned Him, I realized also that whatever the man had planned to do to me, the Lord had definitely confounded him.

The Lord knew the pureness of the woman investigator's heart even though she was involved with the Klan. Realizing that we were to teach her even though we had been told to not go back there anymore, we prayed for guidance from the Lord. My companion, Marina Strong, told me she knew what the Lord wanted us to do in order to share the gospel with this woman. She then proceeded to tell me how I was to park the car across from the people's house away from the property; then, since she was white and could apparently go on the property, she would go get the woman and we would take her to the church and teach her. The plan worked, and the woman did accept the gospel joyously, although her husband did all he could to destroy her feelings of what she knew to be true. Eventually he gave her permission to be baptized with the stipulation that she was never to involve the children nor discuss the Church in their house.

Feeling that her words of love were not enough to express her gratitude, she gave me a T-shirt that read, "Secret Member of the Ku Klux Klan!"

Soon after that experience a man called the church and asked the bishop if he would send some missionaries over to teach his wife the gospel. When we knocked at their door, a woman answered and we told her who we were. She looked shocked as she invited us in and excused herself, then disappeared into another room. Her reaction made me think about the many times my oldest sister had been accepted by letter for an interview for a salesclerk job. When she would arrive, the people would show total surprise and would tell her the job had been filled, and that she should check with the cafeteria manager and see if he needed a cook or dishwasher.

After the woman was gone for what seemed like five or ten minutes, a man walked into the room and looked at us disgustedly. "I asked for missionaries, and not only do I get lady ones, but did it also have to be a set of salt and pepper ones?"

He did allow us to teach his wife, but he made sure he got his remarks in too—not remarks about the gospel, but the color of our skin, often referring to us as "night and day" or "vanilla and chocolate." Many times he would cut me off when I was explaining something about the gospel to his wife, and would ask my companion to explain it. My companion soon realized that it was not because of a lack of clarity that he wanted her to do this, but because he didn't feel that I had the ability to do anything. She then began telling him she didn't know how. He finally settled down and accepted my sharing the gospel with his wife.

We found many persons with this attitude—attitudes that a person's skin color determined his or her intelligence. But we simply rolled with the punches as we accepted the fact that many people in this great country still had a long way to go in their own knowledge and feelings.

As I gradually overcame opposition from the world, my trials began with a few of my leaders. My disobedience to the "be in on time" and "stay in your own area" rules created problems between me and them.

We were to be home by 9:30 each night, and almost every single night we would be involved in teaching a discussion. We knew the rule and we honestly tried to obey, yet we just didn't have the heart to cut a discussion short when the Spirit was so strong. Other times we would be asked to go teach a family that others had tried to teach before, a family that was usually out of our designated area, though there was a rule that we should stay in our own area. Even though we usually ended up baptizing the people, we still got into trouble for having left our area. We wanted to be obedient, but we also wanted to share the gospel wherever we could. So I would simply justify our disobedience by telling myself it was for a righteous purpose.

Not wanting the zone leaders to have hard feelings toward us, we began pulling little playful jokes on them. The mission president apparently heard about the jokes plus our disobedience to the rules. At the next zone conference, he really let us have it.

As I sat listening to him talk to us about being obedient to the rules and to our leaders, I felt both hurt and upset. I felt there were two sides to every story, and he'd heard only one. I then thought about the first time Daddy found out I had stolen some food from one of the local stores. Mama had come outside where I was playing to tell me Daddy wanted to talk to me. Daddy wasn't a man of words, so I knew something was wrong. As I walked in the room, I could see his belt lying across his knee—I knew then that my feeling about something being wrong was for certain!

Daddy asked me if I'd stolen a bag of beans from the store. The way he asked it, I knew he already knew I had, but I still shook my head no. He sat looking at me for a long time without saying a word, and then he said, "Okay, Frances, you can go on back outside." His voice sounded totally defeated and hurt. My mouth dropped open, I swallowed hard as I saw in his eyes the pain my lying caused him. He had always told us children to *never* lie—and *never* steal! He had always said, "If you children can't buy it, don't you steal it!" I had not only disobeyed him, but I had also lied.

Seeing the hurt look in Daddy's eyes, I wanted to admit the truth but I was afraid—afraid he wouldn't understand that I had done it to help out. We had not had anything to eat for two days.

A sick feeling now filled my heart as I realized how Daddy must have felt when one of his children had stolen because he was not able to provide food for us. This feeling deepened as I also realized that I had justified my disobedience then as I had now.

When the mission president finished, he made a comment that started the tears built up inside me flowing. "Though the Lord may bless you to see one soul come into His kingdom," he said, "He might have blessed you with more had you been obedient in all things. For obedience is the *first* principle of heaven."

As I knelt that night by my bed, my tears again began to flow. Instead of praying, I thought back over my life and realized how I had failed to learn obedience as a child and still had not learned it as an adult. I had not only failed my Mama and Daddy in this area, but also the Savior. Feeling a greater determination to be obedient in *all* things, I silently began to pray and to tell the Lord that I definitely would *try* harder to be obedient. Then, as clear as if he was standing next to me, I heard President Spencer W. Kimball's soft voice whisper, "Do it."

My goal after that night was to obey and trust in the Lord to help me and my leaders do what was right. None of us had to feel that we had to have things our way; rather, we should do what was best and right for those we had been called to serve.

A week after the mission president's talk and my setting my goal for obedience, I received a letter of love and support from Elder LeGrand Richards. He shared with me memories of his missions; he also included a tape called "Walk the Highway."

I had been happy in my service to the Lord, but in the weeks that followed, as I applied the advice to be obedient given me by those who cared and understood the importance of doing so, I found a greater happiness.

The Field
Is "Black Already
to Harvest"

5   Days turned into weeks, weeks into months, and
months into a year, and before long, with much sadness,
I realized that I had only a short time left of my mission.
So many people to share the gospel with—and so little
time.

At my last Christmas conference in the mission field,
with only two and a half months to go, I approached the
mission president and asked him if I could please stay for
the full two years. If not, could I at least stay for one extra
month? I told him also of my desire to go labor among
my race before my mission came to an end. He expressed
concerns over my safety in a black area but said he would
let me know. He couldn't give me an answer about an extension until he talked to the brethren in Salt Lake City.

With only a month and a half of my mission remain-
ing, thinking the president had forgotten our talk, I
wrote him a letter.

Dear President Pratt,
    Let's see, what can I tell you about this
week? The area is still here and so are we.

My water fighting days are over. I retired after getting defeated by eight elders.

President Pratt, I am grateful to you and my Heavenly Father for the areas where I've been called to serve. . . . I am truly trying to make you and my Heavenly Father proud and pleased with my efforts. I'm sincerely grateful for my calling as a missionary, though it hasn't been a bed of carnations. Through the rough times I feel I have grown, so I'm not complaining.

I want especially to give thanks for the area I am now serving in. Having been brought up ghetto-poor, and coming here to labor among the rich, carried a deep inner fear for me; I didn't think I would have been able to relate to these people at all, but I've learned a lesson about "richness in the world" and "richness in the gospel." It's been a growing and humbling experience.

President Pratt, I don't mean to complain or hurry the Lord, but will you please petition Him and see if I may labor among my race of people? I honestly know that the field among them is "black already to harvest." Please allow me to serve among them before my mission ends.

If the Lord says no, I will understand. Sure do love you, President Pratt. I am grateful for the love and guidance you have given me. May the Lord continue to guide you as you continue to guide us.

Sister Sturlaugson

A few weeks later the Lord granted me one of my desires but denied me the other one.

In early January, President Pratt called to tell me the Lord wanted me to labor in another area of Texas. He told me there was a large percentage of black people in that area. My heart leaped with joy. Then he told me he had heard from the brethren in Salt Lake City about my extension. When I asked him what they had said, he told me he would forward the letter to me. I thanked him for the new area in which to serve, and hung up knowing my extension had not been granted.

Sleep was impossible that night as I lay thinking about knocking on the doors of black families. The thought came to me to go to every black minister in my new area and ask them if I could talk to them.

Upon arriving in my new area, I shared this idea with my new companion. She then shared with me a dream she had had before her mission. In the dream she had been talking while standing before a large congregation of black people. She felt frightened at first, but then she looked down and saw a black girl. The black girl smiled and gave her a nod of confidence, and her fright vanished. In her dream she distinctly remembered the church as being a little white wooden building.

We decided to put my thought with her dream and find that little white church, both feeling sure that once we found that church we would find a minister inside waiting to let us share our message with him and his congregation.

This area was one of the greatest of my many different areas. Great joy came into my life and my service to Heavenly Father as I saw how the hearts of my race were open to the gospel of Jesus Christ. I was grateful for the way they readily accepted my companion. I had to mar-

vel at the black people's attitudes. Despite all the suffering and hardships many had gone through, they, like
Mama, still held onto the belief in a God in heaven who
loved and cared about them. It didn't seem to matter how
busy they were or how little they had (many of their
homes reminded me greatly of the area and house I'd
grown up in); the minute we told them we had a message
about the Savior and His gospel truths, their doors were
opened to us. It took time for them to understand the
principles we taught and the importance of those principles, but their hearts were pure with a desire to learn.

I thought the issue of the priesthood would hold
many back and, of course, with some it did. For others,
the answer in essence was, "Let the past bury itself, and
let us strive for what tomorrow can be." The older people
especially said that it didn't matter because they knew
they were God's children, and whatever the Lord did was
all right with them, because they knew He did things only
out of love. Hearing many of the older people's answers
made me think about Daddy and the attitude he had had
as he took whatever work he could find in order to take
care of his family. Many times as he was sweeping the
floor in a store or picking up the trash outside, he would
be called names or ordered around, but he accepted it
and kept striving to make a better tomorrow for us.

Though we found many blacks to teach, we still
looked fervently each day for that little white wooden
church. We knew it had to be there, but as each day went
by and we saw many churches except the one we wanted,
our hopes began to lessen.

One day we went to the Rehabilitation Center and
invited some of the workers we had been teaching to
come see a church movie. As we were leaving, I glanced
into one of the rooms and saw a young man with long

hair lying in bed. Quickly I nudged my companion and nodded toward the room. As we walked into the man's room and toward his bed, he turned his head toward the wall.

"You look like you should be tired of lying there doing absolutely nothing. Don't you feel like a waste?" I said. He remained with his head toward the wall. "Well," I continued, "why don't you come see a movie we're going to be showing at our church?" Still no reaction. "Are we too ugly to look at, or is it our breath?" I asked, feeling defeated. As he slowly turned back toward us, a smile began to spread across his face.

"Neither," he said painfully. "I have to say no to your invitation, though. I can't walk."

He then told us about the terrible accident he'd had seven years ago when he was twenty. A tornado had swept through the small town of Hubbard, Texas; and as he ran with his little daughter to the shelter at the neighbor's house, the tornado had thrown them from his backyard into that of another neighbor. From nine o'clock that morning until six o'clock that evening he lay unable to move; in the distance every so often he would hear the weak cry of his daughter. Finally someone found them. He was taken to a nearby hospital, where he was in shock for three days. Then he was told he would be a paraplegic for the rest of his life.

As he shared this with us, I looked at his frail body beneath the sheets. I remembered the way my cousin's body looked before she died. We had been the same age and had done everything together, from winning contests in school to getting in trouble. We both ran track and usually ended in a tie for first place. Then, when we were both a little more than twelve years old, she began to lose her balance. I laughed, and so did the other kids whenever we saw her do it. The stumbling grew worse until she no longer came to school. Eventually she was unable to get out of bed and walk around at all.

One evening I went to see her and noticed that even her speech pattern was becoming slow and her pronunciation of words poor. Each time I asked my aunt what was wrong with my cousin, she'd say they didn't know, that the doctor couldn't find a problem. Nearly a year went by with her body slowly deteriorating.

Finally one evening when I went to see her she was in tears; this was the first time I'd seen her cry since the whole thing had begun. She couldn't utter any words by now, and could barely move her arms and head. Slowly she moved her arm till her hand was pointing at the old family Bible on a table near her bed. I knew she wanted me to read a Bible story to her, but I didn't care for the Bible any more than I did for God, which was absolutely nothing at all. I stood biting my lips and not moving, wanting to cry as I realized she was just like Mama, needing the Lord to sustain her through her trials and pain.

Finally I realized that she wasn't going to stop looking at me with pity and helplessness until I read to her, but instead of picking up the Bible, I yelled at her and asked her how she could possibly believe in some God that was supposed to be so loving and kind, yet all He had done for her was to cause her pain. Tears rolled down her cheeks as she slowly pulled her arm upward to point to a sign above her bed. "JESUS LOVES ME, THIS I KNOW, FOR THE BIBLE TELLS ME SO." As I read the sign and looked back down at her, she was both smiling and crying. That night she died. A year or so later they determined that she had died of sickle cell anemia.

Now as I looked at the young man lying there in bed, I felt grateful to Heavenly Father for preserving his life

40

and giving him the opportunity to hear and accept the gospel in this life.

As we began to tell him who we were, he shook his head and explained to us that he had absolutely no need for God nor for religion. And as for becoming a Mormon, he told us we could show him all the church movies we wanted and talk till we were blue—he hesitated a few minutes as he looked at me—then added "or dark gray"—in the face, but he would not become a Mormon and would never believe in a God.

He proved to be my greatest challenge. With so little time left and what seemed to be a brick wall, I felt totally lost. Day after day we would go to see him, hoping just to become his friend, but he was ice cold to us. Finally one day he told us we wouldn't have to keep coming back much longer, because the doctors had located kidney stones in him again but this time they weren't going to be able to operate on him because his body was too weak. "So my days have become numbered," he said, staring at us with a blank look on his face. "I only wish they had ended for me seven years ago."

Without asking him, we began sharing the plan of salvation with him. I recalled how my cousin had died without my ever having read that Bible story to her, and I realized I was sharing it with him for another reason. That reason was tied to a little fourteen-year-old child we had never completed sharing the gospel with.

We had been on his street looking for someone to share our message with when he'd come riding up the street on his bike. He stopped in front of us, almost hitting us with his bike. He then asked who we were and what we were doing on "his" street. After telling him who we were, we asked if he and his family would like to hear our message. He said he had everything and would listen to us only to find out if he wanted that too. We began teaching him with his mother putting one stipulation on things: *he could not and would not be baptized a Mormon.* As we proceeded to teach him, we were often dumbfounded at his sharp comprehension of the gospel. We watched his excitement as he attended church with us on Sundays and the joy he seemed to have whenever he was in the presence of missionaries.

He called us one Saturday morning to tell us he and his mom were going to visit some of his relatives in another part of Texas, but that he would give us a call when they returned so we could tell him what had been taught in church that Sunday.

When we went to bed Sunday night, he hadn't called. As the week progressed, we were unable to ever find anyone home. Finally, going on the second week, my companion and I decided to go over and try again. We knocked for quite a while before a light came on. A few minutes later the boy's mom came to the door. Realizing how late it was, I quickly began explaining why we were there. I told her we missed her son and wanted to make sure everything was okay with him. While I was talking she began crying; then she took us each by one hand and pulled us inside. She told us how she and the boy had been on their way home that Sunday night and, because it was late, he had crawled across the back seat to go to sleep. That night they had a car accident, and the boy rolled off the seat and hit his head against an object on the floor of the car. He was taken to the hospital, but a few hours later he died.

I had become used to the feelings of growing to love people and then having to leave them when we were transferred, knowing that I might possibly see them again in this earth life. But death was a whole new thing to me. I hadn't lost through death anyone that I'd felt

close to but Daddy and my cousin. This boy had champi-
oned such a close feeling of love in my life, and his death
practically destroyed me. I hadn't realized how much he
loved me until the evening we went to his house to teach
him and learned that he had gotten into a big argument
with some kids at school. Some of them had been making
jokes about black people, and because of his love for me,
he had stood up for blacks. He was a brother to me in every sense of the word and truly had an understanding of
the gospel and the love we were to have for one another.

As I thought how that little boy had been learning
for the eternities, I looked back at the young man lying in
bed and again felt grateful to the Lord for not taking his
life in that tornado. We finished sharing with him the
plan of salvation, and he turned his head away and stared
at the wall. Bearing our testimonies to him strongly, we
told him how much the Lord loved him, and that in due
time all things would work together for his own good.
Reaching out, I placed my hand on his shoulder and told
him to please try trusting the Lord just a little bit; he
would see just how much the Lord truly did love him. "I
don't know why this has happened to you," I said, "but
this pain is only for a small moment, and if you will just
accept the Lord's love and follow him, someday the joy
will far outweigh the hurt you feel now. I promise you
that all things shall and will work for your own good if
you will just have faith in God. I know!" Tears ran down
my cheeks as I recalled how the Lord had helped me in
my life.

For what seemed like hours, the three of us said
nothing; total silence filled the room. "Would you mind
if we said a prayer before we left?" I asked him finally. No
answer. My companion started to say something, but I
shook my head. Again the long silence prevailed. Just as I
felt that we had lost, his left hand moved and he reached

out for us. Both of us reached our hands out to him. "I will," he said. "I will pray."

A few weeks later, he was baptized. Before being confirmed, he asked if the brethren performing the confirmation would give him a health blessing. It was given. A few days later, when we went to see him in the hospital, he smiled a big "guess what" smile as we walked into his room.

"Doc came to see me after my test," he said. He waited a few minutes to keep us in suspense. "No sign of kidney stones. I didn't know God could move so fast," he added with an even bigger smile. He then proceeded to tell us how, lying flat on his back in bed, he was going to teach as many people the gospel as the missionaries would teach out walking around. "Unless they are sister missionaries," he said teasingly.

That night we left him kind of late, both feeling tired but very happy. Suddenly my companion stopped talking and her mouth dropped open. Automatically I turned to look out the window in time to see that we were passing a little white church. She quickly turned the car around and parked in front of it. In the dark we walked up to it. "This is it," she kept repeating in amazement. "This is it!" We searched to see if there was a meeting time. Nothing except the name of the church and the minister's name. We both stood for a few minutes just staring at the church, afraid to leave for fear morning would come and it would be gone.

Each day we drove by that church just to assure ourselves that it did indeed exist. Finally Sunday came, and we could hardly restrain ourselves through our correlation meeting. We left early because we wanted to get to that church the same time as everyone else. When we arrived, cars were already parked and everyone was inside. As we walked in, we could tell that the meeting was well underway. Since my companion was white and very blonde, it was hard to ease in unnoticed. The minister invited us to come sit toward the front. Toward the end of the meeting he asked if we would stand and tell them who we were. Immediately my companion looked at me, and I remembered her dream and nodded my head for her to do the talking.

Very straight and tall, she walked up on the little stand, turned, and faced the congregation. My heart glowed with warmth and pride. She proceeded to tell them who we were, and then she said, "My brothers and sisters," she paused, "we have been sent here with a very important message for each of you. You see, your minister here," she pointed to the minister who was standing next to her, "is a good man, but he doesn't teach you all the truth. He doesn't even know the truth."

Moans and groans could be heard throughout the congregation, and I sat in a cold sweat, wondering what she would say next and how in the world we would ever get out of there. She then looked at me. Again I remembered how in her dream she had looked at a black girl and the black girl had given her a look of confidence, so I gave my best shot of a look that said, "Go on, you are doing great," praying she would say something and say it fast. "My companion will tell you more," she said, as she came and sat down.

It had taken courage to say what she had said, and because of her words many who came up to us as we were shown the door wanted to know why she had made such a statement. This opened the way for us to go to many of their homes and share the gospel with them. One woman from that congregation heard and accepted the gospel and was the instrument for a whole chain of baptisms as she shared it with her immediate family as well as her aunts, uncles, and cousins.

At last, with deep regret, my mission came to an end. As I boarded the plane for Salt Lake City, I opened a letter that Elder Greene, one of the missionaries in my area, had given me. "Do Not Open Till on Plane" was written on the envelope. Inside were words that broke my heart even more.

As I stare out the window,
the tears in my eyes,
I see faces of those I love.
We have just said our last goodbye.
The flight will be long and trying
as two questions plague my mind:
Do I want the life that's ahead
or the one I'm leaving behind?
Eighteen months was such a short time
for going door to door.
As I sit reflecting,
"Surely there must be more."
Is this day truly my last?
"Please Lord, it just isn't fair—
the time goes much too fast!"
As I stare out the window,
the tears in my eyes,
I see sisters and elders I love.
We have just said our last goodbye.
The flight will be long and trying
as two questions plague my mind:
Do I want the life that's ahead
or the one I'm leaving behind?

In God's Eyes

6

As I finished reading the poem given to me by Elder Greene, I thought about how he had been rather distant toward me when I'd been transferred to the area he was in. One day, not liking the coldness that was apparent between us, I confronted him as to why he didn't seem to like me. It took some time for the discussion to finally get going and for feelings to be admitted and dealt with, but we did it. He was very open and honest with me about his feelings for blacks. He shared with me the fact that because of the way he'd always seen blacks portrayed on television and because the few who lived in his hometown lived in poor areas and worked in menial jobs, he felt whites were better than blacks. He shared with me how he had known that the gospel taught that we were all brothers and sisters, but he still felt that whites were better, even in the eyes of the Lord.

As time went on and as he worked with black people, he soon came and confessed his rude awakening. "Man, in God's eyes it doesn't matter what color, earthly positions, or wealth we might have; it's how we live his commandments that counts. The poorest man on this earth could, in a sense, be the richest." After that we had some good talks and were open and seeking to learn from each other. We discussed the priesthood revelation and how many felt it had not been inspired by the Lord. Many had feared for the Lord's temples and what would happen to them if blacks were permitted inside. He and I both agreed on how this was just another way the Lord was "cleaning out his house," and that as time went on, He would do even greater things than that in His church; then those who really didn't know what the principles of the gospel were all about would lose their testimonies. "Can you see what's going to happen in that day? Many will have to take counsel from a black bishop, and they won't be able to do it because of pride," Elder Greene commented. I agreed, sad that this would cause many to leave the Church.

Elder Greene and many others had been good to me as I'd gone through periods of difficulties in the mission field. Remembering those periods of difficulties, I thought about the many missionaries I'd heard using the word "nigger," or making jokes about my race. I realized during those times how close my Heavenly Father was, as comfort would come through the scripture—"inasmuch as ye have done it unto one of the least of these my brethren, ye have done it unto me." (Matthew 25:40.) And I would know that whatever pain I experienced at the names people used to degrade me or others of my race, my Father in heaven and my brother Jesus Christ were experiencing the same pain, because we were His children, too.

I also remembered with sadness the elder who was assigned an area that had a small section that was black, and he refused to go into it because he didn't have "any respect for them people." Though he had never known any blacks, he still had those feelings. He told me that he was prejudiced and probably always would be. I often wondered how such feelings could exist. Each time I looked at how the gospel of Jesus Christ had crumbled a whole brick wall of bitterness and hatred within my own life, it was truly hard for me to understand people who had had that same gospel—some of them all their lives— yet they still retained such attitudes. I would listen as they would say we were all brothers and sisters, yet their attitudes and actions showed something completely different. I came to understand what the Savior meant when he said, "This people draweth nigh unto me with their mouth, and honoureth me with their lips; but their heart is far from me." (Matthew 15:8.)

I sat thinking for a few minutes about Heavenly Father and how people constantly said they love Him. "For he that loveth not his brother whom he hath seen, how can he love God whom he hath not seen?" (1 John 4:20.) I then remembered Mama and her love for people. I recalled the time I'd come home from school furious because my best friend's father had gotten hit in the mouth by a white man who didn't like the way he'd looked at him. As I told my family about it, I was calling whites all the names I could without using any four-letter words. Mama suddenly walked up to me, placed a hand very firmly over my lips, and stared into my eyes. Then, very slowly, she said, "Child, if yous can't think of nothin' good to says 'bout that white man, yous don't says nothin' a'tall." My face flushed dark red with anger as I waited for Mama to remove her hand so I could answer her back. When she finally did remove her hand, tears had formed in my eyes and I thought of how much I hated her. "Mama, why do you stick up for . . ." Her hand immediately went back over my lips. "Child, the good Lord says to teach yous right, teach yous to love one another, to turn the other cheek, do good to those that do yous wrong. I's don't care how many times yous may has

49

to turn yous other cheek, yous jus' keep findin' them to turn, 'cause the good Lord says to do it, and He's will bless yous. Yous got to love, child; yous got to learn thet two wrongs don't make no right. Yous got to forgive and love or the devil will 'stroy yous soul. I's you's mother, and I's to teach yous right no matter how bad it hurts yous."

As she turned to walk away, I continued staring at her, anger and hate boiling through me. I remembered wondering if she knew how her love for the white man and for God was destroying my love for her. I remembered wanting to laugh out loud, to tell her she might as well give up because I would never love whitey nor her God.

Resting my head against the seat of the plane, I realized how much hurt I must have caused my Mama. "Oh, Mama, what a foolish child I was. Sure hope I can someday tell you how wrong I was and how much I love you." I then thought about my brothers, especially my brother Johnny.

Johnny was my favorite. I remembered the time I'd called home from my mission and one of my brothers had answered and wished me dead. Silently I prayed then and now that it hadn't been Johnny, as I recalled the closeness he and I had once had. I remembered the many times I would do things wrong and Daddy would find out, and Johnny would usually take the blame, accepting either the punishment or the beating for me. I thought about the time I'd almost died with pneumonia after standing out in the rain to seek forgiveness from the Lord so the devil wouldn't get me. Johnny, thinking I was going to die, had gone out the next day and done the same thing because he didn't want me to die and be alone.

I recalled the time the dog grabbed the only biscuit I

had (we hadn't had a bite of food, just lots of water, for two and a half days); Johnny was about to take the last bite of his biscuit, and despite the hunger he felt, with tears in his eyes he'd handed it to me and smiled. I thought of the hours we used to talk about what we wanted to become when we were grown, making sure we would have our homes close to each other. And then I recalled the painful memory of Daddy's funeral and how Johnny wouldn't even look at me when I had that feeling of needing him to say, "Frances, it's gone be all right."

As I wiped the tears from my eyes, I knew that somehow I had to see Johnny and talk. "Please, Heavenly Father, just work things out so that somehow I can see Johnny again," I silently prayed. "Please do."

As the announcement came that we were beginning our descent into the Salt Lake Airport, fear began to pound in my heart. What was I going to do? No home. No family. I then questioned Heavenly Father why he hadn't softened the hearts of my family so I could have been flying home to them. "I'm scared, Heavenly Father. I'm so very scared, and I feel so alone right now. What do I do when this plane lands?" Then I thought about Mama. Thinking about the faith Mama had always had in the Lord brought a smile to my face. "Okay, Heavenly Father, I guess faith has to still be my guide. You've brought me this far; I'm sure you're not going to leave me now," I thought to myself as I waited for the plane to complete its landing.

What Now, Lord?

7

The tears were coming faster as I walked off the plane toward the people waiting at the door. I was surprised to find so many people waiting to greet me, yet so very thankful for the arms of love that went around me as each welcomed me home.

The fear of not having a home to go to was soon lessened when one of my companions, Marina Strong, told me her family would love to have me become a part of their family. I hugged John and Analee Strong with deep gratitude for allowing their home to become mine. That night as I wrote in my journal, I expressed to my Heavenly Father my appreciation for blessing me with a loving family and home. "You see, Heavenly Father, I was a stranger, and they took me in; hungry, and they fed me; lonely, and they gave me love. Thank you for fulfilling my needs through them."

As I finished writing, I thought about the time I was getting ready for my high school graduation. Mama had made a dress for me, and she looked at me with tears in her eyes and said, "Child, the Lord does truly provide." As I sat on the side of my bed, I tried expressing my love to Heavenly Father for all he'd done for me. "Seems like all the blessings I've asked of you, Heavenly Father, you've granted me except the blessing of being united with my family again. Yet I know that time will come."

The next few days were extremely busy ones as I rushed about trying to get ready for my homecoming report and to get settled in my new home.

Sunday came much too soon for me; before I knew it the hour had come for me to share my eighteen-month mission to Texas with others. I decided to begin my talk with a poem I had once received from Sarah:

> "If your days were untroubled and your heart always light, would you seek that fair land where there is no night?
>
> "If you never grew weary with the weight of your load, would you search for God's peace at the end of the road?
>
> "If you never knew sickness and never felt pain, would you reach for a hand to help and sustain?
>
> "If all you desired was yours day by day, would you kneel before God and earnestly pray?"
>
> I've asked myself these questions, and the answer is quite plain: I'd seek God less often and need him much less, for God is sought more often in time of distress. And no one, no one knows God or sees him as plain as those who have met Him on the pathways of pain.
>
> Many times since I've been a member of this church, and especially during my mission, I have reflected back upon my life and wondered what I had endured that could

54

be considered my greatest trials. The answer is always the same: losing my family and the restriction of the priesthood to my race. In due time I know things will work out between me and my family. I know they will. As for the priesthood, it wasn't so much the restriction of the priesthood that caused me a lot of agony and pain, as it was the many different explanations I used to hear people giving as if it were sound doctrine. Let me briefly share a few of those many explanations with you. There was once the man who looked at me and said, "Mary, I'm going to explain to you exactly why your race does not have the priesthood." He went on to tell me that everything was a carryover from the preexistence. "In the preexistence," he said, "we all had an opportunity to hear and accept the gospel. But while we were listening to the gospel, your race was off playing basketball! We have come to this earth and we still have the gospel—and your race still have that basketball!"

And I heard such things as that we were "fence-sitters," "less valiant." Oftentimes people would look at me and tell me that the color of my skin was the curse given to Cain, whereas the scriptures so plainly state that the curse given Cain was to be "cut off from the presence of God," and the marking placed on him was a mark of "protection."

As I've spent eighteen months in the service of my God, I do want each of you to know that it really doesn't matter to me what I may have done good or bad in the preexistence; it's what I do now, the same as with each of you, that's going to determine all my eternities.

I want to express my gratitude to our Heavenly Father for giving me the opportunity to serve and to learn more about His truth, for many times He opened understanding unto me. Those eighteen months were definitely hard, but they were also the greatest and shortest eighteen months I've seen thus far in my mortal life.

I'd like to also thank each and every one of you for the love and support you gave me during those eighteen months. I can't say I'm happy to be home, because I'm not. I still long to be in the mission field, to be a full-time missionary for Heavenly Father to my brothers and sisters.

You often hear missionaries say they found out the purpose for their having been called to serve in a certain mission. Each day I kept waiting for that feeling to happen to me; I wanted to feel that I had found and accomplished the purpose for which I was called to Texas. But despite any effort I put forth, that feeling never came.

I had many trying times, but I had a great mission president, great companions, and some truly great brothers and mission couples to serve with. They gave me their all in trying to help me overcome my trials.

You will probably recall that I didn't

want to go to Texas for the fear of coming home in a pine box, but how glad I am that the Lord didn't give me His second choice. I'm deeply grateful for each of the areas that I was called to serve in, and for the knowledge and growth I came to have as I did serve. A man once called my companion and me professional salesmen as his heart was softened toward us and the truth we wanted to share. I told him that the only professional in this work was God. I know that I am nothing without Him.

As I come back to live here, I hope I never lose the title of "sister" and that my work will go on. One woman upon seeing my name tag at the airport, asked me if I was going to or coming from the mission field. When she found out I was leaving, and saw how hard it was for me to do so, she said, "Keep sharing the gospel, honey. Don't let your mission ever end." I pray I never will. I pray that that unfulfilled feeling will remain with me the remainder of my mortal years.

Again I want you to know that I know this gospel is true. If there was the least bit of doubt in my mind that it wasn't, I would be with my family today. You see, I love my family, and it's hard being without them and their love. My brothers and sisters, please pray for our reunion someday. I *know* the power of prayer. I *know* that God hears the cries of His children. When I first joined this church, people often commented that probably when enough of my race joined, we would then probably have the blessing of the priesthood. But I knew that when enough of you, who already had that blessing in your lives, became so concerned and full of love for your black brothers and sisters that you went down on your knees and made your cries of love and concern known to our Father in heaven, the doors would open. You see, it's going to have to be a lot of you and your children who are going to have to take the gospel to my race, and you need to have reached that point of love and concern in order for that to be fulfilled. So I do thank you for the prayers you offered in our behalf then, and I do ask for them now.

To those of you who haven't gone on a mission, I want to say that you really don't realize what you are missing. Eighteen months or two years might sound like a long time, but it's only a speck of a second. I still find myself arguing with our Heavenly Father. Each time I think about the number of years He's given me upon this earth and the number of years I hope He will yet give me, somehow it just doesn't seem fair that He gave me only eighteen short months to be a full-time servant for Him.

There are still a lot of Mary Sturlaugsons left out there in the world. Some are filled with hatred and some are just plain simply lost, and they may not all be of a black skin. But all it takes is for you to say "lean on me; just let me help you to be strong, and together we will return Home!" That's what the gospel of Jesus Christ is truly about.

The road ahead to loving each other as true brothers and sisters is not going to be easy. One of the greatest tools Satan uses is that of hardening the hearts of Heavenly Father's children toward one another. And as long as he can continue to do this, for whatever the reason or reasons may be, he is satisfied, for he has us breaking our Heavenly Father's second greatest commandment.

God lives. He lives, and He loves each of us more than our human minds will ever be able to comprehend. I just hope and pray that we will continue to strive to love each other the way He loves us and wants us to grow to love.

Sarah

8 A few weeks after being home I began writing letters to different people in South Dakota trying to locate my Indian sister Sarah. Each day I hoped and prayed for word from someone saying they had seen her or had some idea where she was, but weeks went by with no word from anyone.

I enrolled for spring term at BYU and, with my best friend Debbie Peterson, moved close to campus. Dad Strong had a phone put in my name in our apartment, which proved to have been inspired.

One evening as Debbie and I were eating, the phone rang. Debbie answered it, then yelled that it was for me. Being completely wiped out from a few games of racquetball and dying of hunger, I asked her to take a message and tell whoever it was that I would return the call. After a few minutes Debbie returned and handed me a piece of paper. I placed the paper next to my plate without looking at it and continued eating. Kevin came for me just as I finished eating, and off I went, still without noticing who had called.

As I lay in bed later that night, I remembered the call and got up to see from whom it had been. No paper.

After searching for a few minutes, I returned to bed thinking I'd ask Debbie about it in the morning.

Just as I was getting out of the shower the next morning, I remembered the call and yelled to Debbie if she knew what happened to that piece of paper. No answer. I came out to find she'd already gone to class.

A week must have gone by before I remembered it again. Debbie looked puzzled when I asked her about it. "Didn't you ever call her back?" she asked. "No," I said. "I couldn't find the piece of paper. Do you remember who it was?"

She thought for a few minutes. "I think she said . . . " She again paused to think. "I'm not sure of the name, but she said she was your sister calling from South Dakota. She wanted you to call her back because she really needed to talk to you."

Before Debbie had finished I was up looking through things, trying to find that piece of paper as I pleaded with Heavenly Father to please help me. We ripped our apartment apart but with no success.

For weeks I waited, hoping Sarah would try again, yet fearing that she probably wouldn't. She was proud, and if she thought someone didn't want to talk to her, she would not pursue the issue, just simply chalk it up as an experience to learn from and go on.

Each day I checked for a message bearing her name or answered the phone hoping to hear her voice, but there was nothing. Then approximately three weeks later, Mom Ellis called to tell me that quite a bit of mail had accumulated at their house for me. I went to pick it up on the way to one of my classes. As I drove, I thumbed through the letters to get an idea whom they were from. At first I wasn't sure my eyes had read one of the return addresses correctly, and I quickly glanced down at the letter again. Sure enough, it did say "Wagner, South

Dakota." While driving I kept glancing quickly at it, as the faint recognition of the handwriting was made. It was from Sarah!

I completely forgot about class, pulled the car off the road, and hurriedly opened her letter.

Hello Mary (or can I still say "sis"?):

Long time no see, no hear from, no talk to. Do we still have a "sister" treaty between us? I am left to wonder, since I called you and you wouldn't come to the phone nor return my call. And even as I wonder, I pray . . . pray that we haven't completely lost the love we once shared.

I guess lots has happened in your life as it has in mine, huh? I'd love to know all you have done. I will now try to catch you up on me and my life.

First, sis (hope it's all right to say that, because that's what I really still feel you are to me), have you heard from your mom? Nearly six months ago I talked to Louise on the phone, and it sounded like Mom was still having a hard time getting over Dad's death. Louise said Mom stayed in her room a lot, and her eyes were always swollen from crying. They have rushed her to the hospital a few times on emergency for her high blood pressure. Louise said she's really had a few close calls. I hope she's better. I wish I could do something for her to make her life a happier one. She's spent most of it suffering. I was trying to save money to send her something nice for last

Mother's Day, but my own situation wouldn't allow me to.

I heard from Louise that Johnny is married and his wife is expecting twins. Maybe if they are girls, he'll name one after you, since you two were so close.

By the way, sis, has the situation between you and the family gotten any better? I sure hope so. I know how hard it had been on you when you were here.

Sarah then talked about the difficulties she had had since we separated. As I read some of the things she'd gone through, my eyes filled with tears. She had drifted away from the gospel, but she constantly bore her testimony of its truthfulness to me.

She talked about how she'd held on to the gospel principles long after we separated, but explained how life on the reservation was a whole different ball game than that in the outer world.

She shared with me things about her past and her family life, most of which she'd shared with me before. She talked about a lack of strength—strength she'd been unable to find, and how the struggles of daily living just plain got to be more than she could handle. She talked about having left the reservation for a period of time, but the racism in the world had driven her back "home." She then began to share about the first time we met.

Then you came, Mary. At first most of us feared you as well as were curious about you. Your color seemed so mysterious. All I knew about black people was gained from one paragraph I read in history that talked about "Buffalo Soldiers."

I don't know how we became the good friends we did which soon led to a strong sisterhood, but I am glad it happened. You were the first person ever in my life who made me feel you cared about me.

We have gone through a lot together, sis. I hope I was able to give some strength to your life and your struggles as you so abundantly gave to mine. We are sisters, and no one can ever make me believe differently. I knew this before the missionaries taught us that we were; they just simply confirmed it!

Mary, I love you and I love the Lord and I am working to be what I know I should be. I won't quit until I have won. Maybe someday I'll be able to send my son on a mission to teach others as the missionaries came to teach us. I just hope he doesn't come across two investigators like we were if he should go!

Hope many moons won't go by before I hear from you, as many did without a telephone call. Please read Philemon three through six and know that I love you, sis, and always will.

Your sis,
Sarah

I sat for a long time staring at the letter and crying, as I realized what a choice sister the Lord had blessed me to have. Sitting there, I tried to remember what I had ever done to deserve her for a best friend and sister. She had been the one who had always given. I owed my very life to her for saving me that time I'd gone outside in a blizzard seeking peace of mind. She had been the one who had stood by me all through the trial I went through with my family. She had been the one who had comforted me after Daddy died. She had been the one who had truly given all the strength.

As I sat there, I thought about the day we had both been baptized and how she had happily hugged me and said, "I'm so grateful, sis, that this life is only a beginning."

As I folded her letter and drove back to the apartment, I immediately got paper and pencil to write Sarah the million thoughts that were in my heart, but all I kept writing was, "Sarah, I do love you."

Going Home

9 A few weeks after I wrote Sarah and assured her of my love, I boarded a plane to go see Mama. I didn't know what was going to happen, but I knew I had to go. The fear of her dying weighed on my mind constantly; I had to let her know that I loved her.

The decision to go home had come after I received Sarah's letter and after I'd called Daddy's sister in Chattanooga. I'd prayed the night before for the Lord to help me know what to do about making contact with my family. I tried calling my sister in Chicago, but she wasn't home. I tried the number of one of my brothers, and it was busy. Finally the thought came to me to call one of the relatives. I tried to get the phone numbers for different relatives but had no luck. I was about to give up when I remembered Daddy's sister in Chattanooga.

When I reached her, she apparently thought it was my sister in Chicago who was calling, since both my sister and I are named Mary. As the conversation progressed between us, I learned that Mama had had a stroke and was in the hospital in critical condition. Midway through our discussion she must have realized, because of my lack of knowledge of what had happened, that I wasn't the

Mary in Chicago but the one in Utah. She then accused me of killing her brother (my Daddy) and hung up.

I felt bad to know that she too felt I'd been the cause of Daddy's death, yet my becoming a Mormon couldn't possibly have caused his cancer. I wondered how many others felt that way about me. "Guess I'm really the 'white sheep' of the family," I thought as I went into my room to pray for Mama.

As I prayed my heart began to pound fast, and the desire to go see Mama became strong. I drove to Springville and shared my desire to go see Mama with Mom and Dad Strong. They assured me of their support, and before the conversation was finished, Dad Strong had my reservations all made and confirmed.

That night was a restless one for me, for I dreamed dreams of being home. The most horrible dream was of my being there and, as one of my brothers tried to shoot me, the bullet hit my brother Johnny and killed him. Waking up from that dream left me shaking and in a cold sweat. I didn't want anything to happen to Johnny. "Oh, Heavenly Father, please help me that things will work out all right when I go home. If nothing more, please bless me to see Mama and Johnny one last time," I cried as I knelt by my bed. I awoke the next morning still on my knees, and apparently I had cried in my sleep, because my eyes were practically swollen closed.

Before leaving, I asked Dad Strong to give me a father's blessing, and I sat listening carefully to every word of counsel and guidance from the Lord. In the blessing the Lord constantly said to "be not afraid," to listen to and obey the promptings of the Spirit, which would guide me during this step in my life as it had in times past. "Remember, Mary," Dad Strong said in the blessing, "the Lord will work things out for your own good and for the good of your family. Never fail to want His will to be done."

I turned and hugged Mom and Dad Strong, thanking them for the love and support they had given me. "Pray for me, will you? I have a feeling I'm really going to need all the prayers I can get."

The Gabbitas, some close friends in Provo, drove me to the airport. They told me a lot of people were praying for me and for my family. As they told me this, I remembered one of the missionary preparation classes I'd talked to at BYU and how that whole class had fasted for me that things would work out when I went home. The Lord truly had blessed me with many friends who cared about me, "Thank you, Heavenly Father," I said, my heart swelling with deep gratitude for all that He'd done for me.

As I sat down on the plane, my thoughts drifted to a million different things. Trying to concentrate on one thing, I opened my journal and began reading it. I found myself unable to concentrate on what I was reading because Johnny kept entering my thoughts. Finally I took out a pen and wrote an entry for Johnny in case something did happen and I didn't get a chance to see him.

To my Precious Brother Johnny,

It is usually impossible for me to express myself verbally to those I am very close to. Therefore, God's given me a poem of sorts so that you might know the fulness of thankfulness and love I have for you. If it shows one thousandth of what I feel for you, I will be happy.

Johnny, though the hands of God have

separated us and guided us to different shores, you are and always will be my favorite brother; that fact will never change.

I will love you, dear brother
beyond eternity.
God's made a home for you and me,
Life's sweetest moments, a fond memory,
For I will love you beyond eternity.

As the plane neared its destination, I tried to shake off the fear that seemed to be closing in on me so strongly, but it was impossible. I then thought of a million things I'd say to Mama, but I knew that if the words didn't come, I'd just hold her close in my arms and let my tears try to convey the message in my heart.

I thought about Johnny and all I'd like to say to him, but more than anything, I wanted to hear him say he loved me and that I was still his favorite sister.

I didn't expect any of my family to meet me at the airport because I hadn't told them I was coming; I was afraid that had I told them, they would have told me not to come. This way, when they saw me I would be there, and whatever happened would just have to happen.

My whole body trembled with nervousness as the taxicab stopped in front of the hospital. I stood looking at the building and recalling the many times Daddy had been there. I thought about the feeling I'd always got whenever Daddy had to be in it, a feeling that he would never come home. Hospitals frightened me. I shivered as I thought about my Mama being in there.

Walking slowly, I entered the hospital and asked the receptionist for Mama's room number. She gave it to me, then explained that it was not visiting hours. I explained to her that I'd flown a long way to see Mama and had only a little time to stay. I asked her if I could please go up ahead of time. "Rules are rules, and they aren't to be broken," she told me rather sternly. Realizing that it wasn't going to do me any good to press the issue, I sat down near a window to wait until visiting hours, which were almost an hour away.

Fear hit me hard as I realized that my brothers would probably be coming to see Mama during visiting hours, and no way would they let me see her. Remembering how Daddy had sneaked out of the hospital when he didn't want to be there, I decided to do the same thing but in reverse. I would simply sneak in! I sat for a few minutes trying to plot my entrance into the hallway. Feeling that the receptionist would notice me if I started toward the hall, I prayed for the Spirit to please help me know what to do. "I know it's wrong to pray for you to help me do something that's breaking a rule, but the ox is in the mire," I prayed. And then, like a miracle, a group of people came in and surrounded the receptionist's desk. I quickly got up and headed for the elevators. As I stepped inside the elevator I smiled in relief and said softly, "Thank you, Heavenly Father." I kept smiling as I thought about Daddy and how he used to escape, and wondered if he had smiled when he'd made it out each time.

I hesitated a few minutes before entering Mama's room. I quickly said a prayer and then pushed the door open and walked inside. I could see a woman lying in one of the beds with her eyes closed. As I got closer, I wasn't sure it was Mama, yet she was the only one in the room.

"Mama," I whispered as I gently touched her forehead. Her skin felt extremely warm, though it wasn't the warmness that made me feel nauseated with sadness; it was the look of her face. Her skin wore lines of defeat even as she lay resting peacefully. Her body looked

71

smaller than ever beneath the sheets. Was this really Mama? She looked so frail and undernourished. Nothing more than a skeleton. Tears formed in my eyes as I stood looking down at her. Before I could wipe my tears away, they fell on Mama's face. Slowly, tired red eyes opened and stared up at me.

"Mama," I again half murmured and half whispered, leaning closer to her face. "Heavenly Father, thank you, thank you very much," I prayed in my heart as the feeling of reality that I was actually seeing Mama touched my heart. As I felt Mama's face next to mine, I cried harder. Then I felt my own face becoming wet and knew Mama was crying too.

"Frances? Is it yous, daughter? Is it my lit' girl?" Mama was asking as if in fear that it wasn't, yet hoping that it was.

"Mama, it's me. It's me, Mama," I repeated over and over to her. She tried to place both arms around me but realized one was fastened to the bed for the fluid that was being given her. With all the strength her frail free arm could give, she held me close and we both cried. "Thank the good Lord," Mama kept saying through her sobs, and she clung to me with all her strength.

"Mama, I love you," I kept saying, sometimes aloud and sometimes to myself, as I gently rocked us back and forth as much as possible.

Finally I eased away and stared at Mama. "Mama." No other words would come. Unable to not be close to her, I leaned back down, pressed my face against hers, and sobbed like a baby. Happiness filled my entire body. "Mama, I've missed you so bad. Please, Mama, assure me that you love me. Please, Mama?"

"Frances," I heard Mama faintly saying. "Lord, thank yous for lettin' me see my girl again." This time it was Mama who rolled back and forth in an effort to rock me in her arm.

"What are you doing here?" The words were said in such a harsh and loud tone of voice that I jumped with fright. Turning, I saw two of my brothers standing in the doorway, staring with both shock and anger at me. I quickly glanced down at Mama, who had fallen into a deep sleep. "What are you doing here?" the question came again as they began to walk toward me. I quickly leaned down, kissed Mama's forehead, and walked out. As I passed them, I felt for sure that one of them was going to grab me, but neither of them did. When I reached the door, I got the strongest feeling that they wanted to stop me, but they didn't. Pride and stubbornness would never allow them to do so.

My reaction must have surprised them as much as it did me. Surely they expected me to react, and, as I walked down the hall, I wondered why I hadn't reacted. Why had I walked out of there without a word of protest or explanation? I asked myself. It then hit me why. I had asked the Lord to guide me every step of the way, and He did. I realized how it was the silent treatment that had always gotten us the most when we were growing up. If someone offered us no explanation when questioned, we would do all we could to reevaluate ourselves to find out why.

I smiled and gave thanks to Heavenly Father for being beside me and guiding me. I felt kind of sad that I hadn't spoken to my brothers, but maybe no words at all had been the best way to handle the situation.

As I was about to go out the door of the hospital, I remembered the note I'd written Johnny. Knowing I probably wouldn't get to see him, I walked over to the receptionist and asked her if she would deliver a note to my

Mama. She explained that it was all right for me to go on up and see her. "Visiting hours started ten minutes ago," she said, as if surprised that I hadn't noticed the time.

"Well, it really wouldn't do me any good to go up now," I said sadly. "My time has run out. I must be going."

The receptionist looked sorry for my being unable to see Mama, and she apologized for not being able to let me go up earlier. "Oh, that's all right," I said. "You have your orders to obey."

I addressed the note to Mama and placed Johnny's name underneath. "Do me a favor, will you?" I asked her as I handed her the note to Mama for Johnny. "Will you please wait until visiting hours are over before you have this delivered to her? I'm sure she will have a lot of visitors during visiting hours, and I'd like for her to be alone to read this note. Also, when you take it up, would you please read what's written here out loud to her." I had to ask her to read it, or Mama would not know that it was for Johnny and could possibly give it to one of my other brothers to read to her.

As I made it outside, I thought about the possibility of Johnny coming to see Mama before I left. I quickly rushed back inside and asked the receptionist if I could add a few more words to the note I'd given her. She handed it to me and again apologized for my not being able to see my mother. I felt a slight feeling of guilt when I saw how she was feeling about the whole situation. I tried to assure her it was all right. I quickly inserted a message to Johnny that I would be at the airport late because I was taking the night flight out. I then included one of our favorite codes—SNY (someone needs you!). We had always used this code when we were growing up. Maybe it would make him remember some of the special talks we'd had.

Hours passed while I waited for my return flight back to Salt Lake City. I paced the corridor praying Johnny would come. "Please, Heavenly Father, I know I'm always asking of you, but please let Johnny come." I prayed and then later added, "If it be thy will." This was really hard for me to add, because in my heart at that time I wanted my own will to be done.

As I waited and prayed, I thought how similar the feeling of loneliness and anxiety was to the time Mama was having a baby and Daddy wasn't home. We all sat around frightened, thinking she was going to leave us for good. We were all so scared, hearing Mama scream and moan in pain. The weather was cold that night, and the old wooden stove gave very little heat in the house, so we sat huddled together near Mama's bed, crying too. Finally Mama told my brothers that one of them would have to go get someone to help. We knew that none of the neighbors knew anything about delivering babies, and the midwife Mama usually had lived in Rome, Georgia.

Frank and Ernie said they would go to get someone. Bundling up in a bunch of old sweaters and socks, they left. Hours passed and they didn't return, while Mama continued to scream in pain. Around midnight Frank, Ernie, and Daddy returned to a house of sobbing kids and a wife who lay completely still. Daddy was covered with dirt from a day of ditch digging, but he went to kneel near Mama and very gently lifted her head. Kissing her forehead, he said, "Lord let her be all right; don't take her from me." I had never heard Daddy pray before, and hearing him do so left me feeling both shocked and scared. Then he wrapped Mama up in a quilt and left with her in the old truck. We all began crying again, feeling certain that Mama had died.

I remember sitting near Johnny and asking him what we would do without Mama. "I don't know, Frances," he said as he stared ahead. "I worry about Daddy," he continued. "What will he do? Mama and him are good friends like we are. He won't have a close friend without Mama. He'll probably kill himself like I was going to do when you almost died because I didn't want to be alone nor let you die and be alone. Frances, what is Daddy going to do?"

Daddy didn't return home that night, and come morning we all grew even more sure that Mama had died and Daddy had gone to bury her. Johnny and I finally went to sit outside in the cold to watch for him. Toward afternoon the old truck drove up. We sat staring at Daddy as he got out of the truck. Afraid, we waited for his news.

"Yo' got another brother," he said. "And yo' mama gone be alright." As Daddy told us the news, we all were happy, though each of us noticed that Daddy looked worried. "What's wrong, Daddy?" one of my brothers asked. "Is Mama really alright or is something wrong?" Daddy sat for a while not saying anything. Then, reaching down and picking up one of my brothers, he said, "Son, I wish I could give yo' Mama a better life. She done gave so much to me. Of all she went through wif this baby, she woke up, reached for my hand, and smiled and asked me if I was alright." Daddy then sat and cried as he held my brother's face close to him.

Remembering that time, I kept wondering if Johnny would remember the feeling we had had while we waited for Daddy's return and realize that maybe I was going through that same feeling waiting for him to come talk to me.

Time came to board the plane. I looked around one last time with one last ounce of hope and knew Johnny wasn't coming. The depressed feeling didn't lessen as it had when Daddy had come home, yet I no longer had to keep waiting and wondering if he was going to come.

I had gotten to see Mama, and for this I was grateful. There was still the pain of not having seen Johnny, yet there was the hope that he would get my note and read it and know how much I still loved him. Sitting there on the plane, I wondered when the day would come when all the desires of a person's heart would be fulfilled. I had wanted to see Johnny and hadn't. I had tried to get in touch with Doug, the white boy who had attended our school, and the numbers with his last name had either been disconnected, were private, or the person answering didn't know a Doug. Resting my head against the seat with a feeling of defeat, I quickly thought about Mama and the few minutes we had had together.

"Where are you going?" someone asked, and from the closeness of the voice I knew the question was directed at me, though I hadn't realized that someone had sat down next to me.

Without looking around at the person I simply said, "Home, I guess."

"Where's home?" the person asked.

I was silent for a few minutes. "Well, they say home is where the heart is, and if that's true, here is home for me. Other than that I really don't know."

Thank You

10

It took quite a while for me to get back into carrying on with my life after having seen Mama and longing to be with her still longer. As the days passed, I worried about her and her recovery. I kept hearing her thanking the Lord for allowing her to see me again. The feeling of how she must have wanted to see me touched me deeply, and I realized a mother's love must be like that of Heavenly Father's.

I still found myself hoping Johnny would try to get in touch with me, for I refused to accept the fact that he didn't love me anymore. Life began to be more hectic for me, as I busied myself with dating, speaking in church meetings, going to school, and working as a counselor for the black students at BYU.

With the constant requests to speak in church meetings, I found it somewhat impossible to accomplish all the things I wanted to accomplish as well as keep up with my schooling and work. Wanting to share the experiences I'd had on my mission with others, I began working on a book about it. I realized very early that something was wrong; each time I attempted to write about my mission, my mind would go totally blank. I tried using the journal approach (a book written through day-by-day happenings), but this would not fall into place either.

One night after lying in bed for what seemed like hours wondering why I was having so much trouble getting started on the book, especially when the experiences were so fresh in my mind, I decided to give it another try. I concluded that if I didn't get anyplace with it this time, I would forget the whole idea.

After I crawled out of bed and sat on the floor, I felt completely awake and alert, and the desire to write about my mission was very strong. I must have written for nearly an hour before I stopped to read what I had written. I honestly couldn't believe what I saw. Everything was about my childhood! I sat, dumbfounded, and stared at the words on the paper. This was *not* what I wanted to share in a book. All I wanted to do was to share about my mission, nothing else.

Crumpling up the sheets of paper, I proceeded to throw them at the wastebasket near the bed. I took more paper to begin again. Nothing. Not two single thoughts would come together. After a few frustrating moments, I put the paper aside and sat staring at the floor. Before long I realized that my eyes were staring at the crumpled sheets of paper near the wastebasket. "No!" I said aloud as the thought came to me to get them and continue with my childhood. "No! That's not what I want to write about." I then got back into bed and turned my light off.

At work the next day I told my boss, John Maestes, about my desire to write a book about my mission. I shared with him the struggles I was having getting started. He suggested that I first tape everything and then have it typed out. Before I knew it he had a tape recorder in my hand and had found an empty room so I could get started.

I sat for a few minutes trying to get my thoughts together, but again, my every thought centered on my life before I joined the Church. This time I decided to follow the thoughts that were pounding away in my heart, though I wasn't sure why or how my childhood life would tie in with my mission.

I had never shared my life with anyone; in fact, the only person who truly knew me was my Indian sister Sarah. As I did so now to a recorder, many times I had to stop, for the hurts of things that had happened before brought sobs that choked my words. The recorder became a friend in a matter of moments, and I shared with it my past pains and struggles to finally find the joy that filled my life now. Within a week I had the feelings of my life recorded, typed by various people (I'm not a typist), and edited by a dear friend. I still didn't understand why I'd shared my earlier life for others to read. As the book progressed toward completion, I simply placed all trust in the Lord, thinking maybe He knew why and in due time so would I. My only desire for the book was that maybe it would benefit someone's life, though I didn't see any way it could. Soon after the book was published, letters began to come to me from people in many areas concerning my talks and the deep appreciation they had for my sharing my life in the book I'd written—letters from people of all ages, such as the ones that follow.

January 1, 1981
Dear Sister Sturlaugson,

Today being a holiday, I decided to catch up on my reading. After considering several books, I picked up a copy of your *A Soul So Rebellious* and began to read. Several hours later, having finished the book, I set it down—filled with emotion. Yours is the most touching story I have ever encountered. It generated within me several emotions, and on three occasions brought me to tears.

I am white, male, age forty, and I also grew up in the South (Wilmington, North Carolina). As I read your book, I was filled with sadness and regret for the way your people have been treated. Personally, I am ashamed for my part in the treatment of blacks in the South. You see, I never put others down because of race, I even felt that I was very accepting of others, whoever they may be, but I was *blind* to the problem.

I would not accept the fact that poverty was real or that your people were really suffering from it or at the hands of the whites. Had I not been so blind to the terrible situation, I could possibly have helped. As has been said, "None is so blind as he who will not see."

Please forgive me and the others like me who, perhaps, could have helped but didn't. Please forgive us who contributed to the problem, whether in ignorance or even through malice.

I was not born into the Church; rather, I converted to it fourteen years ago. I still have to deal with many questions and problems in understanding and accepting the gospel. Your book has greatly strengthened my testimony, and my deepest thanks go to you. I have never met you, but

I love you for what you have done and for what you are.

I know the gospel is true, and I thank our Heavenly Father for sending such a choice spirit as you at this time.

Joseph Chenworth

December 28, 1980

Dear Mary,

My name is Paul. Do you remember when you came up to Heber to give a talk at a morningside for Brother Blanchard's seminary students? I was there listening, and I want you to know now that your talk had a significant impact upon many of my emotions and attitudes. I'm glad that the Lord saw it fitting to give you a talent for speaking so that we could get at least a small idea of your experience.

I run a lot, and the day after that morningside I was running on the roads above my home thinking about you and all you had said. I thought of what a wonderful person you were and of the undeniable spirit about you. I tried to imagine what it must have been like for you while you were my age and how confused and angry you must have felt, but I'm sure I could never really know or fully comprehend it all. I've been undeservingly lucky.

A few days ago my little sister got your book as a Christmas present. I got bored with the day's routine and began reading it. It was so vivid and forceful that I couldn't put it down. I read it through without a pause. This may seem normal, but for me, a below-average reader with little discipline, it was a rare occurrence.

At first I thought of what an injustice it was to give a special person like you all of those disadvantages and woes. I seem to have everything going for me, and this seems inordinate since I'm not an exceptional spirit. But you *are* something more than this. Why was the world's dope loaded up on you?

Then I got to thinking about how happy we were when, before we were born, we learned that we would be tested and tried in "the furnace." I'll bet you were very happy, even though your tests were unusually long and tough (probably even brutal and cruel).

You remind me of the tree that was forced by the dry ground to push its roots way down deep for its water. Then when the winds came, it was able to hold up and stand because of those deep roots. Or you are like the chick that has to scratch its way out of its shell to hatch, making it strong enough to live once it is out of its shell.

Even though I can't really know the kind of pain you've been barreling through, I am glad that you could at least help me with my weaknesses through your example. I am glad for you and I admire you very much. I'm glad I could have a sister like Mary Sturlaugson.

Your friend, Paul Rasband

December 25, 1980
Dear Mary,

My name is Sharla Kae Grover and I live in Kennewick, Washington, on an apple and cherry orchard farm. The reason I am writing is to thank you and somehow express some of the deep emotion I'm experiencing now after just having finished your book.

When I first heard *A Soul So Rebellious* advertised on the radio down in Provo, I was taken with a strong desire to get your book and read it as soon as I could. That was crazy for me, because it was finals time at BYU. And today on Christmas, when everyone is supposed to be napping, I've finished your book and am writing to you —not really knowing what to say but unable to control this strong urge to do so.

Your writing is powerful, as are the experiences you have had to go through. My heart rejoiced and ached simultaneously upon reading your hurt, your happiness, and peace in the gospel, and your strength of spirit. I've not been so deeply moved in a long time and cried to myself continuously as I read—starting with the first chapter. Please accept my thanks to you for sharing all that you are and have become so beautifully. You have deepened my breadth of experience and my capacity to feel. You have shared a world I've never known about and ached to see. You have enlarged my heart toward others whoever they may be. Thank you.

By the way, I'm white and was raised in the West. It's hard for me to hear that people would be the way you described as you were growing up. I wish there was something I could do, but I realize it must start with me and the way I treat *all* of those around me.

I also ached to serve a mission, and I realized that dream in 1977 to the Peru Arequipa Mission as a welfare service sister. I offer a sincere hand of love out to you who have so much within you. I'm amazed at the magnitude of your spirit.

Thank you so much. The book and the story are timeless. But more importantly is the priceless worth of her who wrote and experienced it.

Sharla Kae Grover

January 5, 1981
Dear Sister Sturlaugson,

My husband is blind and a professor at BYU. I have just finished reading your book to him.

I started out not liking you, but we ended up loving you.

I like to think that you have been with your father in the temple and that many of your family will join you in the gospel.

Thank you for sharing yourself with us.

Ken and Kathy Jones

Letters of love and strength. I could have received no greater blessings! Despite the joy the compliments brought, I wanted the people to understand that I wasn't the one who deserved the credit—the Lord did. He was the one who inspired me to write about my life. He knew and understood the reason why, though I doubted Him throughout the whole experience. He had also guided my every word. There had been times when I wanted to share more in detail about a particular incident and my mind would go blank; the minute I continued, the words just flowed. Without Him, no way would it have all come together as it did.

My joy seems never-ending, especially as I have received word that my book was being read by a family in Africa. I wanted to go there on my mission. In a sense, that desire has been accomplished. I have been truly grateful for the response of the people and the heart-warming love they have given in return.

Unconditional Love

11   In late March I was asked to speak at a women's conference at Brigham Young University on a panel with five other women from diverse backgrounds. I was told that a question and answer period would follow. Being given about ten minutes to speak, I wondered what I could share with the sisters to help strengthen our sisterhood in the gospel. An experience of the previous week guided my thoughts.

I had been asked to speak to a group of fourth graders at Hillcrest Elementary School. I had been reluctant, because I really didn't know what to say to them. I also felt that whatever I did share with them, they would not comprehend.

The morning I walked into their classroom to talk to them, I was surprised to discover they had a sincere desire to learn more about my race. I stood for a few minutes just observing them and the looks on their faces. Many sat smiling at me, while others had looks of uncertainty. Thoughts of the Savior came to my mind as I remembered how, in the Book of Mormon, I had read about how He had told the people they were blessed because of their faith, and how now His joy was full. "And when he had said these words, he wept. . . . he took their little children, one by one, and blessed them, and prayed unto the Father for them. And when he had done this he wept again." (3 Nephi 17:21-23.)

The day of the women's conference came, this experience was still on my mind. My heart felt full as I stood before the sisters.

"I'm indeed honored to be here today and to be a part of this great women's conference, a conference filled with the meaning of helping each other, individually and as an eternal family. I pray that the thoughts that I share with you today will be in tune with those of others.

"In contemplating the subject I would talk on, I reflected over my life as to when I came into the Church and how there seemed to have always been an indirect question that I wasn't confronted with but the thought was there. I realized that this unasked question was usually due to people's having feelings of delicacy, while others had feelings of not being able to frame the question correctly. All, nevertheless, fluttered around it. Usually I was approached in a half-hesitant sort of way, or with eyes of curiosity, or looks of compassion and pity. Thanks to a little fourth grader at Hillcrest Elementary School, the unspoken question was finally asked: How does it feel to be black?

"This morning I would like to express my feelings to you as to what it feels like to be black, female, and a member of The Church of Jesus Christ of Latter-day Saints.

"The color of my skin has brought me my greatest persecution and hardest struggles in this life—struggles of simply trying to help people understand that this color is as God-given as any other color. It is not one that was forced on me, but one that I believe was selected by choice. We often talk and teach about 'free agency' in the

90

preexistence and in this life. But we seem to fail to comprehend all that it means, or we comprehend it to a point that is pleasing unto us, or convenient.

"In understanding what needed to be accomplished to help each of us return to our Father in heaven, our brother Jesus Christ said, 'Father, send me.' Each of us saw a plan in which we could also do something to help our brothers and sisters in returning; exercising our free agency, we too said, 'Father, send me.'

"I believe that this color is the one I chose. It is a color that has definitely brought me, at times, more than its share of persecution and suffering from the injustice of others. But thanks to the beautiful principles taught me about the gospel of Jesus Christ, I am able to bear the trials of my skin color and not feel bitterness; rather, my heart is filled with sorrow for those who do not have the understanding of these principles in their lives, or for those who do have them and yet lack an understanding of them.

"Our Heavenly Father took great joy and pride in making the many colors and kinds of flowers, trees and fowls in the air, and other things to beautify this earth. He took an even greater pride and joy as he placed his children of all colors upon this earth. We often fail to enjoy the beauty of being his children because of skin color. I witness this often when people confront me and ask me what they should call me—black, colored, Negro, or what. When in doubt as to what to call me, simply call me 'sister.' Do not let the color of my skin hinder you from the knowledge of our eternal bond.

"Being a female has definitely brought about its share of struggles, because it's inseparable from the color of my skin; thus it has seemed to bring with it an automatic reputation of low morals. It still amazes me how in this day and age, people are not sensitive to the fact that we do have feelings and specific goals and expectations. Oftentimes people will see a black man come to BYU and automatically believe that the black man and I should get married just because of skin color. Sisters, did you not have specific qualities in mind when you found your eternal mate? So do we all!

"Being a Mormon has simply given me the greatest of all comforts through my trials of being black and female. For, you see, to know the will of God is the greatest knowledge; to suffer the will of God is the greatest heroism; to do the will of God is the greatest achievement; and to have the Lord's approval on your work is the greatest happiness.

"Being black, female, and Mormon is a struggle, but struggle is the primary law of life. We struggle and we survive. We fail to struggle and we perish. Our salvation is in our own hands, in the stubbornness of our minds, and in the tenderness of our hearts. The task is ours. The strength to accomplish that task is the true gospel of Jesus Christ. As members of his true church, we are the rulers and the ruled. We are the peacemakers and the peace-abiding. We are the beginning and the end."

After the conference we were assigned rooms for the question-and-answer period. As the questions progressed from my mission to my personal life, a woman in the back of the room asked if I felt it would be difficult for me to find someone black to marry, and would I ever marry someone white. Before she finished, I reflected on the racism I'd seen and been a part of as I was growing up in the South.

I thought of the many times I'd watched black men and boys being sent to jail for "eyeing" a white woman; some had even been beaten to death, yet a white man could do the same thing, or even worse, to a black woman and nothing would be done about it. I thought about the many times I'd watch white men hold a door open for a white woman and slam it in my Mama's face. I thought about the times a white person would call another white a degrading name simply because that person had said something kind about a black person. I thought about how I had been shown disrespect by white men.

Then I recalled the time I said *no more!* It had been when I had been in a store to buy a piece of bubblegum. A white man walked right in front of me and paid for his items as if I didn't exist. After paying for them, he stood carrying on a conversation with the cashier, every so often turning to look at me and laugh. Feeling anger in me reach its peak for that day (because the same thing had happened earlier in another store to Mama), I stepped back from the man, aimed that piece of bubblegum at him, and let it go as hard as I could. Then I took off, hoping he would chase me, because if he did, I was gonna lead him right to where our old truck was parked with my brothers in it. He yelled, "You little dirty black nigger," but he didn't follow.

Looking at the group of sisters seated before me, I remained silent for another moment as I silently asked Heavenly Father to remove the anger that was slowly creeping inside me. I tried not to let the tears of frustration fall that were forming in my eyes because of all the injustices I, as well as Mama and the others I loved, had gone through because of people and their lack of love, all because of their reactions to the color of skin.

"Since learning about the true gospel of Jesus Christ and coming to *know* the Savior," I began slowly, "I know that He has an unconditional love for all of his children. I am striving to become like Him in every sense of the word. He does not place a limitation or restriction on His love because of skin color and neither will I. When I marry it will *not* be because of a person's color. He will have to love the Lord, love and live His gospel principles, and love me. If he fulfills those three requisites and if I love him and it's right with the Lord, then I will marry him. In the celestial kingdom, there is no such thing as color. I know that for this life I could please and be accepted more by society and the world if I abided by their conditions and would recognize color first. But in the end it's not society I will have to face for my decisions and choices, but my Savior. Therefore, any decision I make will be with eternity as my goal and Him as my judge.

"So in answer to your question, I can only say that I don't worry about finding a husband on the basis of color. That's not important to me and my eternity."

Before I could finish, a woman spoke up. "Yes, but what about the persecution you would go through if you married someone white? And don't forget your children. How could you possibly put them through something that will be because of *your* decision?"

I paused a moment and stared at the floor. "Ma'am," I said finally, still looking down, "if I seek my Heavenly Father's confirmation for decisions I make and He gives it to me, then I don't care what I may have to go through—I will follow. The greatest persecution a person can go through is that persecution from those one loves most. At least for me that's true. Those I love the most are my family, and because of this gospel I have gone through persecution from them. As I said earlier, when the Lord tells you something is true and accepted by Him, it's up to you to either accept it or do that which would be easier.

"I won't fool myself into thinking children of an interracial marriage won't have their share, plus more, of problems in this world, but oh, how nice it would be if everyone who was so concerned about the children would teach *their* children to have the pure love of Christ. Then my children wouldn't have any problems. You might say parents can only do so much but how much is so much? I often think about the two thousand stripling warriors and who they credited their faith to when they went to war—to their mothers. They said, 'Our mothers taught us.' If we taught our children strongly in the way of love, wouldn't we truly have a Zion?

"If there's an area I know that needs strengthening in my life, it's love, and without that love I will never attain the celestial kingdom. Heavenly Father will never, never tolerate negative attitudes one toward another in his kingdom. I don't fear what the world can or will do to me and my children. It's my Savior I fear. I'm so thankful for people like our prophet, President Spencer W. Kimball, who knew the criticism he would probably get from the world in announcing that the Lord had told him about giving the priesthood to *every* worthy male member of the church, but he obeyed the will of his Savior. I'm grateful for Joseph Smith and the persecution he was willing to go through for you and for me so that we might have the fullness of the gospel. I'm grateful for my brother Jesus Christ for all he went through for us that we might be able to return to our Heavenly Father. And as for my own life and what might happen to me or what I might have to go through, I will do it if it's what my Savior would have me do and not the world."

Lying in bed that night, I thought about all that had been said that day. I felt grateful to the Lord for His love for me, and I made Him a promise that no matter what I had to go through in this life, if it would help in the building of His kingdom upon this earth, I would do it.

Less than a month later, I played racquetball with John Eyer, who was to be my eternal mate.

"Should we?" John said, breaking into my thoughts.

"I'm sorry, John," I said. "I didn't hear your question. Should we what?"

"I'd like for us to have a word of prayer. We are almost to where your family lives. Is that okay with you?"

"I'd love to," I said, as I looked at him and realized the good, strong man God had blessed me to have for a future eternal mate. "I love you, John," I said. "And I am really proud of you for your love and courage."

"I love you, Mary," he said earnestly. "I fear your family in one sense and in another I don't. I know the Lord will be with us and that His will will be done no matter what the desires of our hearts might be. Thank you for loving me. I'm the one who's really blessed, and I hope I can live up to all that you and the Lord expect of me." He took my hand in his as he exited off the freeway to find us a quiet place to pray.

I smiled to myself as I reflected over all that had happened since John and I had begun dating. Though we both were dating others at the time we met, we each knew at the end of our first date that it was not going to be the last one. As we continued dating, the pieces began fitting together. Many times we'd begin discussing an experience and would have to stop as we'd each realize we *had not* shared that experience in this life.

As time passed and our relationship grew, I knew I had to try to tell my family. I finally decided to call Louise, my sister in Chicago. In an effort to get a conversation going between us, I asked her various questions but nothing developed. Finally I told her I'd called because I really needed to talk to her or Mama or someone. I then told her about my feelings for John. She didn't interrupt while I talked. When I finished there was complete silence. Finally she asked, "What color is he?"

Hours following our conversation, John came over,

and as we were having dinner, the phone rang. It was Louise.

"Frances, how can I reach this John?" she asked rather coldly.

"What's wrong, Louise? Why do you want to know how to reach John?" A frightened feeling slowly entered my heart. The thought that maybe my brothers were going to find John and do something awful to him made me feel sick inside.

"Just tell me how or where I can reach him," she repeated rather impatiently. "He can tell you why afterwards if he wants to," she added.

"He's here," I uttered slowly. "Would you like to speak to him?"

"Yes," she said, again rather impatiently. I laid the phone down and walked back into the kitchen where John was. He noticed right away that something was wrong. I told him he was wanted on the phone.

"Who is it?" he asked.

"My sister," I said, in a puzzled tone of voice.

When John returned to the kitchen, he looked dumbfounded. "It was your mom," he said. He then told me what had been said.

I sat for a few minutes saying nothing. Then I slowly went into my bedroom and wept. It hadn't mattered to Mama what color John was; all she wanted was to ask him to assure her that he would keep me close to the Lord.

Within a month, many things had taken place in our lives. John's dad had flown to Utah and taken us to dinner, and John had written a letter to his mom about us. He had later written another letter with a note on the back of the envelope that said, "Guess who's coming to dinner?"

"Is this good enough?" John asked as he stopped on a side street near a housing complex.

"I think so," I said, still smiling from my thoughts of his letter to his mom. I then bowed my head, and before he began the prayer, I silently said,

The Lord is our shepherd;
We shall not want.
He maketh us to lie down in green pastures:
He leadeth us beside the still waters.
He restoreth our souls:
He leadeth us in the paths of righteousness for his name's sake.
Yea, though we walk through the valley of the shadow of death,
We will fear no evil: for thou art with us.